How The Catholic Church Is The Same and How it is Different from Other Christian Churches

SECOND EDITION

by
Franklin J. Dailey, M.D.

DEDICATION

This book is dedicated to the most exceptional and loving woman that I have ever known, my mother, Mrs. Rose Mary Boukal Dailey, and to her children, my brothers and sisters.

And to my loving wife, Florence, who encouraged and consoled me in this and many other endeavors.

And to my son, John, and his lovely wife, Sandy, and to my grandson, Michael. They are a joy to my life!

ACKNOWLEDGEMENTS

A very special acknowledge-ment to my nephew, Mr. Michael Wourms, who laboriously trans-scribed most of the contents of this book from a tape I recorded at a lecture I gave at a Pre-Cana class.

And to Mrs. Helen Jackson and Paul Giem, M.D., and my best friend, Mr. Walt Abraham, who helped critique the contents.

Also, my thanks to Tom Balboa, Joe and Barbara Bonadiman for their editing of this the second edition.

FORWARD

Dr. Franklin J. Dailey

Dr. Franklin J. Dailey, became deeply concerned because many of the young people he cared for as patients were dropping away from the Catholic Church.

In talking with these youngsters, he discovered they did not know their faith despite the fact that many of them had been through twelve years of Catholic schooling.

How could this be? Dr. Dailey looks at the reasons:

In the years before the Vatican II Council, the Catholic Church hierarchy was strong on memorizing church doctrine and the do's and don'ts of being a Catholic. These methods produced good practicing Catholics, but many had very little understanding of where the Church teachings came from, the Bible, or of the development of Catholic doctrine and practices.

What was accomplished through the memorizing and the do's and don'ts was good and necessary, but what was NOT accomplished – learning and understanding Scripture and tradition – led to a Church catastrophe. After Vatican II, when many external, traditional practices were changed, and certain doctrines were challenged, many knew not the words of our Lord in scripture, "and were washed away" (Matthew 7:21-27).

In this Post-Vatican II period, confusion became so dominant that some teachers "threw out the baby with the bath water." They were not teaching the doctrine and the do's and don'ts, nor were they teaching the Bible and Tradition. Some used their "feelings" and "experiences" to create dogma and situational doctrine, and they reduced the Bible to mere human "experience."

Consequently, young people were left with no roots to anchor them, no compass to guide them except their own experience. In fact, Salvation history was turned back 4000 years to before Abraham!

Some people in both Catholic and Protestant churches went so far as to deny that the Holy Bible is revelation from God through man; rather, they contend, it is merely the "experience of the author or the faith community." They deny original sin and the redemption by Christ, they deny the necessity of Baptism, they deny the physical resurrection of Christ, and they even deny that the commandments must be obeyed.

It is all too apparent where their "non-teaching" and liberal attitudes have led us as a society, resulting in broken homes, promiscuous sex, abortion as a form of birth control, homosexuality as an accepted way of life and, as a consequence, runaway venereal disease and AIDS.

At the same time, in the Church we see the open rejection of authority and prayer life, an unwillingness to accept sacrifice and "to take up His cross" — resulting in a critical loss of vocations and the loss of souls to Satan.

So called "dissenting" theologians cause scandal and confusion when they promote ideas that are contrary to Church doctrine. "They do not serve Christ, but their own belly" (Romans 16:17). Those who follow them would be wise to listen to the words of I Timothy 6:20:

"Avoid the profane talk and foolish arguments of what some people wrongly call 'knowledge.' For some have claimed to possess it, and as a result they have lost the way of faith."

Professing to be wise, these dissenting theologians "have become fools" (Romans 1:22). They promise freedom, but they themselves are slaves of corruption — by high-sounding words (2 Peter 2:17-19), teaching instead the "precepts of man" (Matthew 15:8), disguising themselves as apostles of Christ, but actually serving as angels of Satan.

The dissenting theologians have set themselves up as an alternative authority, rejecting and opposing the authority Christ established; these haughty men will not be swayed by "pastoral council" or gentle coaxing. The way back from this moral confusion, THE ONLY WAY BACK, is to teach what Christ taught the way that He taught it, and to remove all clergy, religious or others who refuse to so teach.

Would this be interfering with academic freedom? A person on the street may argue and teach that the world is flat, but would a university tolerate a science teacher who would teach such a fallacy? Would removing him as a science teacher be interference with academic freedom?

Should a theologian who teaches what is NOT Catholic doctrine be allowed to teach in a Catholic school as a "Catholic" theologian?

"Anyone who does not stay with the teaching of Christ, but goes beyond it, does not have God. Whoever does stay with the teaching has both the Father and the Son. So then, if someone comes to you who does not bring this teaching, do not welcome him in your homes; do not even say 'Peace be with you.' For anyone who wishes him peace becomes his partner in the evil things he does" (2 John 9-11).

Today, in many of our churches and schools, many who have not the doctrine of Christ are made welcome. When we allow them, we share in the evil that they do.

The intent of this book is to inform and encourage the faithful to rise up and support the Holy Father and those clergy and theologians who represent him and Church doctrine and to resist those who are serving confusion and dissension in Christ's Church.

But those who choose to challenge these false teachers should be prepared to be ridiculed and spat upon because "their magisterium of liberal theologies" is far less tolerant and far more chastening than the Magisterium of the Roman Catholic Church ever was. But if you are chosen to be one who is ridiculed and persecuted for His name sake (and teachings) – rejoice, for yours is THE KINGDOM OF HEAVEN. (Matthew 5:10,11)

HOW THIS BOOK CAME TO BE

One evening in the Emergency Room at our hospital, I sutured a laceration on the head of a pretty little six-year-old girl. On her chart, I noted that her father was a minister, so I said to him, "This will heal just as Christ is our personal Savior."

He replied, "Oh, are you a Protestant?"

"No," I answered, "I am a Roman Catholic."

"You Catholics believe that Christ is your personal Savior?" he asked.

"Yes," I said, "the Catholic Church has been teaching that for almost 2000 years,"

Then he asked, "But are you Catholics allowed to read the Bible?"

"Yes," I answered, "the Catholic Church has been teaching the Bible for almost 2000 years."

He replied, "I did not know that. What other truths do we share?"

So, I outlined below the beliefs that we Catholic Christians share with our brother Christians.

WHAT ALL TRUE CHRISTIANS BELIEVE, INCLUDING CATHOLIC CHRISTIANS

1. God is Master and Creator of all things.
2. God created us to share all that He has.
3. The Bible is revelation from God, revealing who He is, who we are and what we must believe and do to share His Kingdom.
4. Man separated himself from a touching relationship with God (original sin), and of himself, had no way to return to God.
5. The Jewish religion was the one true religion until Christ.
6. Christ came to fulfill and sanctify the Jewish religion, and to further teach us what we must believe (faith), and how we must conduct ourselves (morals) to be in His family.

Christ came to give us definitive and authoritative guidance, to sanctify us, i.e., to cleanse us of all sins.

7. There is only one way for us to be united to God, and that one way is Jesus Christ! With the cross on our church, the crucifix on our altar, and each time that we make "The Sign of the Cross" over our bodies, we proclaim that Christ Crucified is our one and only and personal way of salvation.

After I outlined the beliefs that we share with our brother Christian's faith, the minister then asked, "Then what are the differences?" I replied:

THERE ARE NO DIFFERENCES, BUT, IN ADDITION TO THESE BELIEFS, ALL TRUE CATHOLICS BELIEVE:

1. Christ extended His own Priesthood through His twelve apostles and their successors, in an unbroken line, for a continuing close, touching relationship to Him (John 15:12-21; John 20: 19-23).

2. Christ instituted certain signs which, when combined with "the Spirit," would establish or strengthen a very special personal touching by Jesus ("born of the water and the spirit"), and receive an outpouring of His love (grace) into our souls.

All Christians accept that this personal touching and sanctification occurs through a "sign and the Spirit" in the Sacrament of Baptism. The Catholic Church recognizes additional "Sacraments" for the purpose of spiritual healing, nutrition, confirming our relationship with Christ, starting our families, dedication to His service, and at our death.

3. Christ established an authority (St. Peter and his successors) "upon" whom He promised to found His Church and make decisions so that is would be "one fold and one shepherd." "All may be one, as the Father and I are one . . . perfected in unity." (Matthew 16:16-20; also see John 21:15-17; John 17:20-23; John 10:17)

Discussing the beliefs of all Christian churches, and the additional beliefs of the Catholic Church, is what this little book is all about. My hope is that everyone, even the staunchest non-Catholic Christians, will find something in this book to strengthen his or her own faith in Jesus Christ as Lord and Savior, because Jesus Christ is the Alpha and the Omega – the beginning and the end!

TABLE OF CONTENTS

INTRODUCTION

A PILGRIM'S JOURNEY

Welcome to an exciting journey!

In the following pages, you will become a Spiritual Pilgrim - searching, traveling, and looking for a better home. The Pilgrims who came to America in 1620 landed at Plymouth Rock: They were looking for a better place to live, as were the pilgrims who laboriously traveled west across this country back in the 1800's.

Today, we too are pilgrims, traveling through this life, looking for a better home. And your today is the tomorrow you were thinking about yesterday.

One day, as you near the completion of your own personal journey, you will realize that many years have passed which, at one time, was your future.

Everything in your life is something that is coming and will have come to pass.

Everything except one thing: when you enter into the next life.

That will not be a temporary stay; it will be your permanent home; you will never again be a searching pilgrim.

To help you get to your permanent destination, it is vital that you have a map; to get there, you must know where your are going.

For example, let's say I was in an accident and you were kind enough to stop and help me. To express my appreciation, I handed you a gold coin, worth about 500 dollars.

Of course, you would be pleased.

But suppose I said to you, "I have a thousand more of these same gold coins buried under the northeast corner of the Red Dog Saloon in Creede, Colorado. If I die, I want you to have the treasure."

Then, the next moment, I died.

What would you do?

You probably would not even go home to pack! You would go straight to Creede, Colorado!

But where is Creede, Colorado?

It is a little Wild West town. The man who killed Jesse James was killed and buried there. It is north of Durango, Colorado, by about one hundred miles. It sits way up in a canyon and you do not get to Creede by accident. If you arrive at Creede, that is the place where you wanted to go!

You will never pass through Creede, Colorado, accidentally.

To get to Creede, you need a map.

Well, the kingdom of God is a place where I want to go. It is the place where searching, spiritual Pilgrims who travel through this life want to go - but you need a map to get there.

Is there such a map?

Yes.

THE HOLY BIBLE, SACRED TRADITION AND THE CHURCH.

These form the divine map. The Bible is God's written word, Sacred Tradition is the oral teachings of Jesus and His Apostles which were written down by their disciples, and the Church, which is the pillar and foundation of the truth (1 Tim 3:16). With these as our guide, and the promise of Christ at the Last Supper that He would send the Holy Spirit to guide the Church for all time, God has provided all the information that we need in order to serve Him faithfully and to be found worthy to spend eternity with Him in heaven.

If you have not seriously looked at God's map in the past, or, if you did not understand that map, then perhaps this book will help you.

We spend so much time preparing ourselves for this life and so little for the next.

In my own case, I went to high school, four years of college, four years of medical school, and four years of specialty training - 24 years of study – just so I could go out and earn a living in this life treating patients as a doctor!

But the much more important question is, **"How much time have I spent in preparing for my next life?"**

Hopefully, this little book will help motivate you to spend more of your time properly preparing for the remainder of your journey as a Pilgrim's through this life in preparation for the next.

You may also find in following God's map on this journey that the journey itself, your life, will be more directed, enjoyable and fulfilling!

May God richly bless you as you begin your journey!

Franklin J. Dailey, M.D.

1 - DOES GOD EXIST?

How do you actually know there is a God?

After all, why do you want to spend your life as a Spiritual Pilgrim thinking about somebody if He is not even there?

So, we start with this basic question.

"Does God exist?"

That is the question I started to ask in my youth. I questioned and probed, seemingly driving the priests and nuns crazy with my constant questions. The question of God's existence was far too important for me to sit back in a classroom and simply say "Yes" to everything I was taught.

So, I said, "Prove it."

Down through the centuries, many theologians and philosophers have wrestled with this primary question. St. Thomas Aquinas came up with five reasons why he believed that God existed. Some people have fewer reasons and still others have come up with many more.

After years of study, thinking, and questioning, I came up with the following reasons why I believe there is a God: The Creation of the World, Miracles, and finally, Fulfilled Prophecies.

Let us take a closer look at each.

1) **God Exists Because Of Creation.**

A few years ago I was on a plane going to Denver, Colorado, and a young man was sitting next to me. I said something to him about God.

He responded, "I'm an atheist."

I said "Really? Then tell me, how did all of the universe get here – the moon, the stars, the planets?"

"Oh, well, some unknown force created it," he responded confidently. "Science acknowledges it; it's a scientific fact. The universe started out as a big mass and then it exploded out into the space."

I then asked, "Who made the mass?"

"Well, some force," he replied.

"Okay, I'll accept that," I answered. "Was it an Intelligent force?"

"I suppose so," he responded. "If there is an intelligence to the universe, then I suppose it must have come from some sort of an intelligent force."

"Well, that intelligence is God," I summarized.

He said, "That's God?"

1

I said, "Yes."

Like it or not, that is about all our minds are capable of knowing about God. We cannot conceive anything more about God except that there had to be an intelligent force of creation – and God is that force.

You either believe the intelligent force was God or you must believe that a big unknown mass somehow had intelligence, and there is no scientific evidence that any form of mass in our universe has ever demonstrated one degree of intelligence.

Anything else we know about God is because of what He has chosen to reveal to us. Our minds do not have a high enough level of intelligence to comprehend much about God's nature except that which He decided to share through revelation.

Do you have a dog? Could you ever teach your dog to speak the English language? Of course not. He does not have that high level of intelligence. Could you ever teach that dog the value of the gold coin?

No.

A dog cannot comprehend much more than a few basic instincts and commands.

Yet, the dog lives in our world and we talk to him and do things with him, but his level of intelligence and understanding cannot begin to approach that of a human being.

Man is obviously much more gifted than any dog; man is the most intelligent life known on planet earth. Yet, our highly developed intellects cannot begin to parallel the intelligent force Who created this vast universe!

Even if your I.Q. is over 200, and you are a member of Mensa, you do not have the level of intelligence necessary to understand the complexities of God. He has existed from the beginning and will live forever. There is no intelligence on this earth that can ever comprehend that type of nature.

Our finite minds do not like to admit this sort of limitation but, until we are able to create our own universe out of absolutely nothing, we must conclude that an intelligent force far beyond anything our finite minds could ever comprehend created matter!

An atheist is an atheist because his human mind cannot comprehend this; he rejects what he cannot understand! Yet, he accepts electricity, which no human mind can fully understand! He accepts it because of what it does, i.e., its effect.

Once a student told me, "I cannot accept the concept of eternity."

"Did you ever go out in the night and look at the stars in the sky?" I asked.

He said, "Yes."

I asked, "Do you know how many stars there are?"

"No, I have no idea," he replied.

"Neither does anybody else," I told him.

In the book of Genesis, in Chapter 15, God discusses the stars with Abram. God selected Abram to become the father of His people, so He changed his name to Abraham, which means, "honored father of the multitude."

But before God changed his name, He said, "Abram, go out in the night and look at the stars in the sky. Can you count them?"

Abram said, "No, Lord."

God said, "No man can count them."

And to this day, even with the highly sophisticated satellites and modern scientific instruments at our disposal, no man has ever been able to begin to accurately count all the stars in the sky. The Milky Way alone is estimated to contain some 400 billion stars all moving in a complex and orderly fashion.

God said to Abram, "I have chosen you to be the father of my nation and your offspring will be like the stars in the sky. I hereby change you name to Abraham."

The farthest star that I know about is approximately ten billion light-years away. Our sun is just nine minutes away by light traveling at 186,000 miles a second. If it takes nine minutes for the sun's light to get to earth, imagine how far out those stars are that are ten billion light-years away!

And after you go past that last star, how much farther can you go into space?

Science does not know.

High-powered telescopes have captured pictures of colliding galaxies about 50 million light-years away. The Hercules cluster of galaxies is estimated to be in excess of 30 million light-years distant.

We do know that creation is of such a magnitude that no man can truly comprehend it and that no "accidental force" could have created it.

I believe God made our universe so large because He wanted

3

it to mirror a minuscule part of the magnitude of eternity. We will never comprehend eternity, but viewing the magnitude of our universe helps us understand the immensity of our God.

In my heart, I know God exists because of what I feel. In my mind, I know God exists because of creation.

Even modern science agrees that everything on this planet was not always here and that it had to start somewhere.

I believe it started with God, the intelligent force of creation.

2) **God Exists Because Of Miracles.**

What is a miracle?

I was giving a talk in Rudolph, Wisconsin, a few years ago, and the priest asked me to speak to a class of six-year-olds. My approach in speaking to youngsters is to talk with them the same way I talk with adults; so, I explained to them that "There is a God because of creation, miracles, and fulfilled prophecy."

Then I asked this question, not expecting the profound answer I received: "Does anybody here know what a miracle is?"

A little girl popped up her tiny hand immediately and I thought, "Boy, am I going to get a good one here from this little six-year-old."

I said, "Okay, honey, what's a miracle?"

"A miracle is something that can't happen but does happen," she replied.

Theologians could not give you a better definition.

A miracle is something that cannot happen in the natural order; it must happen by supernatural means. We know there is a God because all through both the Old and New Testaments there are miracles that prove the presence of God.

We accept that Christ is God because of His miracles. Had Christ not performed any miracles, had He not risen from the dead, we would not believe He was God. It would not matter that His thoughts and the writings about Him were beautiful and insightful.

Christ is God, and He proved it by His miracles! By instantly healing lepers, by turning water into wine, by driving out demons, by bringing the dead back to life, by walking on water, by His resurrection.

And miracles still go on in our world today!

Throughout the centuries, as in the time of Christ, God always sent His messengers to give warnings, especially when people were headed in the wrong spiritual direction. Usually, the message would say, "If you do not turn back now to My way, something is going to happen."

If the people did not then return to the ways of God, something did happen, just as He promised. If they returned back to the way of God, He blessed them, such as in Chapter 3 of Jonah:

"God saw what they did; He saw that they had given up their wicked behavior. So He changed His mind and did not punish them as He had said He would" (Jonah 3:10).

It is no different now.

If His people are going away from His direction, He will send a messenger again, and that messenger will have a miracle.

This happened on May 13, 1917, when Christ sent Mary, His Mother, as a messenger. Mary visited three little children in Fatima, a small town in Portugal. In 1917, the world was at war.

Mary said, "I am going to give a message to you to give to the world."

The children said, "But we are just little kids."

She said, "Do not be afraid. I will give the people a sign so they will believe."

She appeared to the three children five times over a period of five different months. These children went through many personal persecutions because of these visions. Other children made fun of them, taunting them for their claims to have seen visions.

At one point, they were even jailed.

The children told Mary, "The people in our town are making fun of us; they are giving us a lot of problems."

Mary said, "A miracle will occur that will prove that this is a message from God. On the 13th day of October of this year, God will perform a miracle at one o'clock in the afternoon at the Cova."

And the word spread over much of Portugal.

On the 13th of October, about 70,000 people (including journalists, dignitaries, etc.) gathered at the Cova to see whether the miracle was going to occur. It rained all morning long right up until exactly one o'clock, when Mary said the miracle would take place.

Exactly at one o'clock the rain stopped. The clouds parted, and the sun seemed to go back and forth in the sky, and then, it suddenly seemed to start falling upon the people. The spectators fell on their knees. The government had sent people to disprove any pos-

5

sible fraudulent event, and yet the government agents were on their knees with the others.

Just as suddenly, the sun went back into the sky. Then God said, "I'll do it twice to prove it."

A second time, the sun seemed to come upon them. Those in the crowd thought it was the end of the world. But the sun went up into the sky, leaving everybody miraculously stone dry. They were soaked and wet one moment, and dry the next.

Many people who had illnesses were healed miraculously.

The message from God was proved by a miracle, and miracles prove that God exists. Many books have been written about Fatima, and it is suggested that you read about Fatima, because if the message and events are true, then it is God's revelation in our day. God gave us no new doctrines at Fatima; instead, He chose to remind us once again, as He has done so many times through history, to repent and pray and return to His

Holy ways. Those who attribute the miracles and vision at Fatima to be the work of Satan must read Matthew 12:22, and 37 where Christ was accused of being "the prince of the devils." His answer there certainly applies here.

3) **God Exists Because Of Fulfilled Prophecies.**

All through the Old and New Testament, God performed miracles and issued prophecies to prove that future events were coming from the hand of God.

It is impossible in this book to document all the prophecies that are recorded in the Bible; there are more than 200 concerning the birth, life, death, and resurrection of Jesus alone!

To help illustrate the point, the following list five prophecies are here for you to look up in your Spiritual Pilgrim's journey:

1. Jesus Christ was to be born of David's family:
   The prophecy: Isaiah 9:6-7
   The fulfillment: Matthew 22:42-46
2. Jesus Christ would be born in Bethlehem:
   The prophecy: Micah 5:2
   The fulfillment: Matthew 2:6
3. The side of Jesus Christ would be pierced:
   The prophecy: Zechariah 12:10
   The fulfillment: John 19:37
4. Jesus Christ would rise from the dead after three days:
   The prophecy: Psalm 16:1-11
   The fulfillment: Acts 2:25-32

5. Jesus would be betrayed for 30 pieces of silver:
   The prophecy: Zechariah 11:12-13
   The fulfillment: Mathew 27:9-10

These and the many other prophetic declarations in the Holy Bible demonstrate that, without a doubt, God does exist, and can prophetically predict, with one hundred percent accuracy, the history of man.

Prophecies continue in our present day; they happened again in 1917 at Fatima. The prophecies given at Fatima were:

1. World War I would soon be over. That prophecy came to pass.
2. If people did not repent of their ways, another world war would come during the reign of Pope Pius XII. At the time of this prophecy, no one even knew there would be a Pope Pius XII, yet it was declared in prophecy that he would reign when World War II started. It happened!
3. Lucy, one of the children Mary appeared to at Fatima, accurately told the Pope when World War II was going to start.
4. Mary told the three children that Francisco and Jacinta Marto both would die within two years of her appearance at Fatima and that only Lucy dos Santos would remain to give Mary's message to the world. Francisco and Jacinta did die within the time frame God gave to Mary, and Lucy continues to live, becoming a nun in Spain.
5. Mary declared that if the world did not repent after World War II, God would allow the evils of Communism to spread throughout the world. Today, more than half of the world is enslaved by some form of Communism, including more than one billion people in China alone!
6. A yet to be fulfilled prophecy was that if God's people still do not repent, He will allow Russia to chastise the entire world.

Remember this: in 1917 Russia did not have the power to chastise even Riverside, California. If ultimately, we are chastised by Russia, whom do we blame? The president of the United States or of Russia?

No, we will have only ourselves to blame.

Us.

Mary said if we will repent, say the rosary, and come back to the ways of God, there will be no war with Russia; instead, God will convert Russia. But, if we do not repent, and turn back to the will of the Lord, we will be chastised by Russia. Then, after that, Russia will be converted. Is this danger now over?

Probably not.

The result of this final prophecy is in our hands (just as with the people of Nineveh in Chapter Three of Jonah.)

In summation, we know there is a God because of creation, miracles, and fulfilled prophecies.

There just is no reasonable explanation for these three phenomena except that THERE IS A GOD!

Incidentally, we declared war on Japan on December 8, 1941, the feast of the Immaculate Conception of Mary; and we signed the documents ending that war with Japan on August 15, 1945, the feast of the Assumption of Mary. Coincidence that the war predicted by her would start and end on the two major feast days of Mary?

In summary, the message at Fatima contained:

1. No new doctrine.
2. The message was identical to that of the Bible: repent, pray, accept Christ as Savior, and sin no more.
3. A massive miracle given by God to prove that this was a message from God through His spokesperson, Mary. The miracle was that of the sun seeming to fall out of the sky; miraculous healing of the lame and the sick and the immediate drying of the earth and people, having been soaked with rain only moments before. This witnessed by about 70,000 people.

2 - IF GOD EXISTS, WHY DID HE CREATE YOU?

If you are like most of us, you have often wondered "Why did God create me?"

Let's answer that question with another question.

Did you really want children when you first got married?

Perhaps not.

Because, among other things, you knew there would be diapers to change, clothes to buy, medical bills, and lots of worry.

If we were left to just the stark realities of raising children, many young couples might decide not to have a family.

But there is so much more to a child than the daily problems.

Children enable you to share yourself with others. They enable you to love somebody, and to receive love in return.

Why did God create you? Same reason!

Because God wanted to share Himself, to show His love, and to have someone like you to love Him in return.

But if God just placed you in heaven, your life would have little meaning. To make it meaningful, God had to give us a free will and an opportunity to choose.

So God created the entire universe to give you a place to be born and to grant you the opportunity of making a choice to spend all eternity with Him or to spend it somewhere else.

While on the earth, you have two primary choices – God or the world. We choose the world in place of God when we use the world for the sake of the world, not for the sake of good and of God.

In this world, everything God created is good. When we use things the way God intended them to be used, that is good.

For example, in marriage, when we have sex with our spouse, that is good and pleasing to God. He intends for us to have sex in marriage and to enjoy it.

So what is bad?

Bad is misusing the things (gifts) God has given to us.

When we have sex outside of marriage – as in homosexuality, masturbation, fornication and adultery – that is abusing God's intended purpose for the gift of sex and it becomes "sinful."

The same principle applied in other areas.

When we eat and gorge ourselves (gluttony) until we become sick, it is sinful.

When we eat as we should, to nourish our body, that is good

and pleasing to God.

On your pilgrim's spiritual journey, the first question to ask yourself in any situation is "Am I using these gifts the way God intends them to be used?"

The second question to ask yourself comes from a Protestant minister who told me one day, "In whatever you are doing, ask yourself if Christ could come and join you or bless what you are doing?" Your answer tells you whether it is right or wrong.

The Bible and the Church help you separate your emotions from what you "feel" is right or wrong to that which God has "revealed" to us as right or wrong, and we must always place Gods word over and above what we feel, or our "experience."

God said to respect our bodies and respect our relationship with each other. It is when we abandon ourselves to the things of the world that we separate ourselves from God. If we do not respect and use properly the things that God has given us in this life, what do we deserve in our next life?

Once a person asked me, "What is judgment going to be like?"

I said, "Well, it might be something like this. God may have two pictures of you: one of what you could have been, and one of what you are. He will show you these two pictures. You will see with whom you will spend eternity."

Does a deer run with wolves? A snake knows that he must crawl in the bowels of the earth with other snakes. No one has to tell these animals what they are.

So what do we have to be afraid of?

God?

No.

We should be afraid of ourselves and our choices.

What is God doing all the time we are choosing?

God is calling, Come to Me. Let Me cleanse you, let Me purify you, let Me make you better then what you are.

Three days after I told this story about spending eternity with others like yourself, I got a call from one of my students.

"Is it Church doctrine what you said about judgment? Is that the teaching of the Catholic Church?" he asked me in a rather frantic, worried tone.

"Well, the Church does teach we shall be rewarded for that which is good, and punished for that which is bad," I replied. "Why do you ask?"

"My wife hasn't been able to sleep for three nights," he told me. "Why?" I asked, somewhat puzzled. "What did I say to disturb her sleep?"

"Well, she's a chronic complainer," he told me, "and now she's afraid she'll spend all eternity with other complainers."

We got the message across, didn't we?

What could be worse than an alcoholic spending all eternity with other alcoholics, slobbering and vomiting over each other?

Or an abuser spending eternity in the company of other abusers?

Remember, Christ's words, "I did not come to judge you" (John 12:47.) "I came to save you."

God in His love could not condemn a person, but in fairness to justice, He may allow a person to see themselves for what they ARE and then they judge themselves.

Follow The Divine Road Map –

God gives us a map to use. He tells us what to believe (faith), and what we must do (morals).

But how do we know the Bible is the true road map, the true Word of God?

The same way you know that God exists – through creation, miracles and fulfilled prophecies. Miracles and fulfilled prophesies are many – both in the Old and New Testament.

One word about the Bible before we proceed.

None of the New Testament was written until about 30 years after the death of Christ. By that time, there were churches all over the known world and they were established without a New Testament. How were they teaching? The Apostles were teaching only what Christ had orally passed on to them.

The Church did not come from the Bible rather the Bible came from the Church.

The Church was founded, structured and sanctified by Jesus Christ and He appointed His twelve apostles to be the instruments of bringing His Church to the world. He promised that He would send the Holy Spirit to inspire and guide His Church for all time (John 14:16; John 16:13-15). Again, the Church existed long before there was the written word, which we call the New Testament.

Thirty years after the Church was born (Pentecost), the apostles began writing down what our Lord said and did. This was done for future generations as evidence of what the Church was actually teaching. That is why the Catholic Church can say, "Yes, the Bible is God's Word because we produced it."

In addition to Scripture, we also go back in Church history and discover how the early Christians understood what was being taught at that time. "We teach, not in words taught by human wisdom, but in the learning of the Spirit" (1 Cor. 2:13).

This teaching process is called Sacred Tradition.

Tradition can never be in conflict with Scripture; it is simply another source of information. Tradition goes back into the history of the Church, into what was being taught 2,000 years ago.

We Catholics turn to the leaders of the Church, who are the successors of St. Peter and the apostles, for complete understanding. We go back to the earliest Church and say, "This is what we understood then, and this is what we understand now."

Catholics accept the Bible as God's Word. This is documented in the Catechism of the Catholic Church 105ff.

We also accept the authority of Tradition – the teachings of the Church at the time of the apostles – to help us understand what was actually meant by what Christ taught.

Tradition, then, in this sense is restricted to only the time when the apostles lived. What the Church is – Church dogma, Church structure and authority; priesthood; sacraments – all have not changed in what they are and what they do since the death of the last apostle.

At various times, there have been changes in "the way" or "the application" of doing things, but there have never been changes in "what is done" nor can there be!

By the way, what we accept as "the Bible" today was not put together and authenticated by the Church until about the year 400 AD So, if we accept the Bible as "the Word of God," we must first accept that the Holy Spirit was active in guiding His Catholic Church in this endeavor.

Also, we must remember that there was no printing press until the fifteenth century. During this 1,500 year period, the Holy Words of the Bible were reproduced by hand, carefully guarded, and passed on by the Catholic Church! So if we respect the Bible as "God's Word," should we not have a respect for the Catholic Church "the instrument used by God" to bring to us this revelation?

If we are to accept what comes from an authority, must we not first accept the authority from which it came?

3 - THE BELIEFS CATHOLICS SHARE WITH OTHERS

We all believe that God is the Master of the universe and created all things. That there is one God in three Divine persons – the Father, the Son, and the Holy Spirit.

That God created man in His image and likeness, and that which is man, that is his intellect, conscience, free will and soul was created by God and did not evolve from some lower animal.

We believe that the Bible is revealed truth from God.

We believe that the Jewish faith was the one true faith of God until the time of Christ. Christ did not institute a new religion, but rather He fulfilled and sanctified the Jewish faith.

"Do not think that I have come to do away with the Law of Moses and the teachings of the prophets. I have not come to do away with them, but to make their teachings come true" (Matthew 5:17).

When man sinned, he separated himself from God; man, of himself, had no way to return to God. God gave man the way to return by becoming man Himself, in the person of Our Lord and Savior Jesus Christ.

Christ is our personal Savior, and the only way of salvation.

We can be saved through faith and faith "alone." With Catholics, this faith "alone" must include the "Total Christ," ALL of His teachings, His authority, and His ways and means of sanctification.

"Not everyone who says Lord, Lord, shall enter my kingdom, but he who does the will of My Father shall enter the kingdom of God... He who does not hear my word . . . and follow it . . . will be washed away and utterly destroyed" (Matthew 7:21, 26, 27)

Those are the basic teachings of all true Christian churches, and they are also the teachings of the Roman Catholic Church.

1) A review of the beliefs that all true Christians share

We all agree that God is Master, and created all things.

We agree that the Bible is the revealed truth of God, and we know the Old Testament is true because Christ Himself proclaimed it to be true. If we believe in Christ, then we believe the Old Testament is truly God's Word.

We know the Jewish faith was the one true faith in the time of

Christ. You must be a Jew (in the religious sense) before you can be a Christian.

I have an accountant who is a Jew. When I was having my taxes done a few years ago, he said, "Frank, you and Florence (my wife) should go to the Holy Land. Many things will have meaning for you there."

I said, "Vick, they would ALL have meaning for me."

"What do you mean?" he asked.

"Well," I replied, "I'm a Jew."

He said, "Frank, you're a Christian."

"I know, Vick," I answered, "I am a Christian Jew: I have to be a Jew before I can be a Christian. For instance, Vick, if you decided to become a Christian tomorrow, what would you change?"

He said, "I don't know, what?"

"Nothing. Absolutely nothing," I answered. "You would still believe in Moses and the prophets and all of those things that happened before. Christ didn't come to change, He came to fulfill (Matthew 5:17-19). All you would say is "Christ is the Messiah. He has fulfilled all that was promised'."

2) Original Sin

When man sinned in the Garden of Eden, he separated himself from God; we call this "original sin." Man, of himself, had no way to return to God. Perhaps the most demonic, satanic teaching is that there is no original sin. Satan would like Christians to believe that, but that is not the teaching of Christ and His Church.

If there were no original sin, then there would be no need for redemption, and hence, no need for a redeemer!

Bishop Fulton J. Sheen gave a marvelous explanation of original sin. He described how, in the book of Genesis, when God created Adam; he was created in the image and likeness of God. Adam had a perfect body. He was not subject to disease, colds or sore throats. He was not subject to death (Genesis 2:17).

But, most important, Adam could stand in the presence of God. He could talk with God as you and I talk with each other. When Adam sinned against God, he lowered himself, and the level of humanity to where it is now (Genesis 3:23).

This is the same thing that happened to Lucifer. Lucifer was an angel created by God; Lucifer was given eternal life, yet Lucifer chose to rebel against God's authority (Isaiah 14:12). Lucifer and the other rebellious angels who followed him destroyed their rela-

14

tionship with God by attempting to overthrow Him, so they were separated and forever banished into their own evil kingdom. Adam experienced the same thing. Through original sin he descended into a lower level of humanity. He became subject to disease and death. He could no longer stand in the daily presence of a visible God.

3) Sin Caused The Separation

Can sin exist in the presence of God?

No.

So God said, "I created you to spend all eternity with me. But now you have lost that right."

When Adam sinned, he lost the right to have a touching relationship with God; he did not have a divine inheritance to pass on anymore, so his children are born without that heritage, therefore of themselves, have no way to come into God's kingdom. "And no one has ascended into heaven, except him who has descended from heaven: the Son of man who is in heaven" (John 3:13). So where were Moses, Abraham and the prophets who were pleasing to God up until the time of Christ? They had to be in a place of waiting. Scripture tells us that Christ died and descended into hell "in which He went and preached to those spirits that were in prison . . ." (1 Peter 3: 19-20). This makes it quite clear that there is a place between heaven and hell, and that these souls were alive and aware (not in a state of suspended animation), and that they had to accept Christ as Lord and Savior and put their sins onto His cross to be washed clean in His blood. "Lazarus, the poor man, was "borne away by the angels into the arms of Abraham" – not into heaven because heaven had not yet been opened. Even Abraham could not enter into heaven until his sins could be washed away by the blood of Christ! (Luke 16: 19-33)

Original sin is not so much something you are born "with," rather it is something you are born "without" – without this touching relationship with God! Any time we do not have this touching relationship with God, to use another expression, we are "in sin." This is what St. Paul is saying: in as much as Adam sinned (separated himself from God), we are all born "in sin," i.e., separated from a touching relationship with God (Sanctifying Grace.) Adam no longer had it; therefore, he could not pass it on to his children!

Adam lost his inheritance but God still wants man to spend all eternity with Him, so God instituted a plan so that man could regain his heritage.

God could have given it back through a bolt of lightening but He is not that kind of God. He wanted a personal relationship with us, so God became man. He came down from heaven and became one of us. He knew what it was like to have a headache; to feel depressed, to experience the pain of sharp nails penetrating His hands, to laugh and to cry.

God became man through our Lord and Savior, Jesus Christ. There is no way back to God except the way God had given us through Jesus Christ.

Think of it this way: God is on one side of a canyon (sin), and man is on the other side. What kind of a bridge will it take to go across that canyon of sin, separating man from God?

Man cannot bridge it.

Only a person who could be both God and man could bridge it! Only Christ!

Christ had to be truly God in every way that God is God.

He had to be man in every way that man is man, except in sin.

Only a combination of God and man could bridge the canyon between humanity and Deity. A debt to God could be paid only by one who is equal to God, a person who is God Himself, and yet also a man, two natures, yet one person, Jesus Christ.

There is only one bridge.

Jesus Christ is that bridge.

There is no other way to have ourselves cleansed, to have ourselves purified, to have ourselves redeemed and welcomed back into God's graces except through Jesus Christ crucified, and His Church.

The whole marvelous structure we call "the Church" exists for one purpose: to bring all that is Christ to us and us to Christ and then unite us all together as the family of Christ. Our relationship to each other is far more intimate than just community; we are family, brothers and sisters in Christ. Then we can say, "Abba, Father."

And that is the way we think of God, as a loving Father waiting to guide us, help us, cleanse us, purify us, and bring us into His kingdom. All He asks from us is that we accept Him, love Him, and try to follow His ways.

When Christ became man, He became the way of salvation.

4) Why did Christ die on that cross

For our sins!

But what does that mean?

When you sin, usually you take something that does not belong to you.

If you have sex outside of marriage, you take something that does not belong to you. If you took a gold coin from a neighbor in a robbery, it does not belong to you.

So you owe a debt.

How long do you owe it?

Forever.

In this life and into the next life, the Lord said in Matthew 5:25:

"If you owe a debt in this life, pay it in this life, because if you don't you'll be delivered to the judge who will deliver you to the jailer and you'll be put in jail until every last penny is paid" (see section on Purgatory in this chapter for further explanation).

Every debt must be paid; justice demands it!

However, another person can pay a debt for you.

Since God is a loving Father, He provides a way for His children to have their debts paid for them.

This is what Christ did for us on the cross.

He gave Himself to pay our debt. He let them put nails into His hand; let them put a crown of sharp thorns on His head; allowed them to put a sword in His side; He let them kill Him to pay our debts.

He did this for each one of us personally!!!

Many Catholic and non-Catholics say, "Christ is my personal Savior." Christ did not come to save all the people in the world, or any specific group, He came to save each one of us Personally.

We cannot go to Christ as a group or even as a community.

We have to go to Christ personally. All of the sacraments are on a one-to-one touching relationship with Christ.

Now, where do we go to pay our debt?

If you want to pay your electric bill, you take it to the electric company. When you owe a debt to God, where do you take it?

Where was the debt paid?

Where do we take our debt?

TO THE CROSS.

There is no other place. Your sin cannot be paid except on the cross. You cannot take your sin and throw it out into space. You have to hand it to Christ personally, on the cross. St. Paul said, "We must nail our sins to the cross." (More on the blood of Christ later.) I do not pray, "God forgive my sins" anymore. It no longer has meaning to me. But I do say four simple prayers before I go to bed each night; they take about three minutes.

I pray: "God, be patient with me, I'm a sinner like anybody else; Christ, please take the burdens of my sins and put them onto Your holy cross to be washed in Your holy blood. Lord, I ask You to remember my loved ones who have passed on; and God, whatever is best for my soul, for the souls of my family, I want to happen."

I never question what God does. My prayer puts the responsibility in His lap. "Whatever is best for our souls, God, I want it to happen." If my son is driving down from Bishop (a town in California) today, can I pray he gets here okay?

No, I cannot.

I pray for what is best for his soul. If it is best for his soul that he dies on the way, then I want him dead on the way.

Yes, I will grieve. But I put it in God's lap; "Whatever is best for our souls, God, I want it to happen."

What else can you pray for? That is all there is.

5) The Passover And The Cross

In the Old Testament, the Jews were enslaved by the Egyptians; that is why you hear Israel-Egyptian war talk even to this day; the Israelites were enslaved by Egypt for five hundred years.

They prayed for deliverance. Moses prayed for deliverance.

God said to Moses, "Moses, I've selected you to go tell my people I'm going to get them released."

Moses said, "But-but-but who sh-sh-shall I say that sent me Lord?"

That's right, Moses stuttered. Isn't that interesting? God selected a man to go in front of the king to represent His people, and the spokesman He selected stuttered severely!

Why would God do this?

God always uses the unlikely messenger. If Moses could move mountains with his speech, and the Jews were released, then the Jews would say, "Moses got us released."

But if Moses could not even speak a complete sentence, and the Jews get released, who got them released?

God did.

At Fatima, God did not talk to the local Bishop, or to the Pope. No, God spoke to three little children.

18

Now, how could they get the message? Where did it come from?

Only from God.

So Moses goes in front of the Pharaoh and says, "Look, you release my people or I'll change the waters of Egypt into blood." Pharaoh did not release them so Moses took his staff and struck the waters of the Nile and the waters turned into blood. This impressed Pharaoh.

God performed ten other great miracles (Exodus, Chapters 7 through 12).

After each miracle, He hardened the heart of Pharaoh so that He might perform other miracles to prove beyond a doubt that He was their God: the plague with flies; the plague of the locusts; the plague of the shrimp; the boils on the animals and all the people (except the Israelites); the hail that dropped from the skies and burst into flames when it touched the ground.

What was the last miracle performed to release the Jews?

God said, "Tell Pharaoh, unless he releases all My people, the first-born of all Egyptians and their cattle shall die this night."

So Moses told Pharaoh.

And Pharaoh said, "Show me."

So Moses went to his people and said, "Take a lamb, it must be perfect, you kill the lamb, prepare the meat for a flight into the desert because we'll be leaving tomorrow. Take the blood of the lamb and put it on the doorpost so it can be seen from the outside because this night an angel shall go over all of Egypt and any house that has the blood of the lamb on the doorpost, the angel will pass over that house when he sees the sign of the lamb's blood."

He will pass over that house (that is why we call this event the Feast of the Passover). Any house that does not have the blood of the lamb on its doorpost, the angel will kill the first born in that house. It happened as God foretold.

So the Jews were saved by the blood of the lamb.

And we, too, were saved by the blood of the lamb, Jesus Christ. Jesus said, "I am the Lamb of God."

This is important to our soul. They were saved by their faith, but the sign had to be present (each Sacrament has a sign which must be present). What would happen to a Jew if He said, "Look, I have faith, I see no reason to paint blood on my door post." What would have happened to his first-born?

19

Would we be willing to risk it?

What happens to a man today who says, "I don't believe I have to have water put on my head in baptism, I have faith."

Jesus said, "Unless you are born of the water and the spirit, you shall not enter My kingdom."

Are we willing to risk it?

God asks so little of us, but He demands that the signs be present so that we understand what is happening in our relationship with Him, and that we accept Him as our Creator as well as our loving Father.

6) How are we saved

The blood of the lamb of God; that is why at every Mass the priest holds up the consecrated bread and wine and says, "Behold the Lamb of God, who takes away the sins of the world." (Rev 1:5 "To Him who loved us and washed us from our sins in His blood" and Rev 5:9 "and redeemed us for God in His blood.")

The book of Revelation discusses how God will gather all of the souls on judgment day. He will say to Satan that he may have all of those who do not have the sign on their forehead.

Satan will ask what the sign is?

The Blood Of The Lamb, His name and the name of His Father on their foreheads (Rev 14:1) "We must have our robes washed in the blood of the Lamb, and made white" (Rev 7:14).

"Any soul who has the blood of the lamb on their forehead, you may not have them, they belong to Me."

Satan may not have us unless we wash it off.

How do we wash it off?

By sin ". . .and by sin we receive the mark of the beast on our forehead and upon our hand... and shall be tormented with fire and brimstone forever and ever" (Rev 14:9-11)

When we sin, we wash off the blood of the lamb. Now, if we stand in front of God on judgment day, and we do not have the sign, who gets us?

Here is an illustration.

If I take a one-ounce gold coin down to a pawnshop, they would probably loan me about $200.00 on it, and I would receive a redeemer slip. Anytime within the next 60 days I could pay the $200.00 plus interest, and the broker would then give me back the gold coin. He has possession of it, but he does not yet own it. Now, if I fail to redeem the gold coin within sixty days, then he no longer just has possession, he owns it, and may do with it what he will! The same is true within the spiritual realm.

When we are in serious sin – adultery, fornication, murder, abortion, etc., — we have delivered ourselves into the judgment of Satan. He has possession of our soul. He does not own it yet, but he has possession. At any time before our death, we can go to our blessed Lord through the Sacrament of Penance (confession) and say, "Lord, will you redeem my soul with your blood? Will you pay my debt?"

Through the priest He says yes. Please come to Me. Please bring that burden to Me. Please put that burden on the cross. I will take it, no questions asked. The thing He asks is that we try and sin no more and have sorrow for our sins.

In our weakness we are likely to sin again, but as long as we continue to try, we are continuing in the life of Christ; we have the mark of "the Blood of the Lamb" on our forehead. The only time that we are lost is when we abandon ourselves to sin, and give up and do not try anymore. No matter how great or frequent a sinner we are, Christ is waiting to take us back if we will only try. "For God sent not His Son into the world to condemn the world; but that the world through Him might be saved (John 3:17)."

But if we do not accept Christ, if we do not accept His words, there is someone who will judge us. "He who believes in Him is not judged; but he who does not believe is already judged" (John 12:44-48) and has his mark, the mark of the Beast, on his forehead and hand.

That someone is Satan. (John 12:44-48)

When we are in serious sin, we deliver our soul unto the possession of Satan. If we die in this state, Satan will not only possess our soul, but he will own it. It is his. Christ doesn't want Satan to possess us. He loves us. He created us to spend eternity with Him. What we must do is to place our burdens on His holy cross and try and sin no more.

God commanded the Jews to celebrate the Feast of the Passover every year. I asked my Jewish friend if he still celebrated the Feast of the Passover. He said that he did, every year. I told him that we celebrate it everyday; that every Mass is the celebration of the Feast of the Passover, as fulfilled by Jesus Christ at the Last Supper and continued in His Crucifixion and Resurrection.

21

4 – SACRAMENTS

Catholics believe that sacraments are an integral part of our personal relationship with Christ. Jesus Christ instituted sacraments as "the way" to establish our relationship with God.

All of the Sacraments have signs. They must be present for a valid Sacrament. Just as blood had to be smeared on the doorpost for the Jews to be saved; they were saved by their faith evidenced by the sign of the blood of the lamb. This is the way God provided for their firstborn to be saved; He did not give an alternative way! Nor did Christ provide any alternate ways other than the sacraments through His apostles and the Church.

The word "sacrament" means "a sacred moment" – a sacred moment when you are touched by the person of Christ. Christ wants to have a touching relationship with you. He does not want to be a God "way out there someplace," but a loving, personal, touching God: this happens in the "sacraments."

We know that Christ is present in our life even as this book is being read, so why a sacrament? It is similar to this.

If I call my wife before I go home from the hospital, my voice is at the home, my wife is at the home, but I am at a phone in the hospital. She does not have a touching relationship with me during the phone call.

The spirit of Christ is in the room where you are reading this book, but is it His person touching you?

No. Certainly not in the fullness of a "sacrament."

Stop and think for one moment.

Just as a "sign," the "blood of a lamb," had to be on the doorpost of the Jews at the first Passover (this is the way God provided), so Jesus demanded a sign be present for each sacrament so we can understand what is happening.

NOTE: Sacraments of the living are those which we may receive while living in the family of Christ; i.e., the Holy Eucharist, Confirmation, Matrimony or Holy Orders; Sacraments "of the dead" are those which bring us into the life of Christ, i.e., establish or re-establish our family relationship with Christ: Baptism, Reconciliation, and the Sacrament of the Sick.

1) Baptism And Confirmation

Either as a baby or an adult, through Baptism we are adopted into the family of Christ and given all the privileges and blessings of being in the family of God. Confirmation "confirms" our relationship with Christ. The Holy Eucharist establishes a blood relationship with Christ and continually nourishes this relationship. Penance re-establishes this relationship if we have separated ourselves through sin. Matrimony unites man and woman to a life-long relationship to each other and consecrates this relationship with the family of Christ. Holy Orders consecrates a man's life totally to the service and extension of the Priesthood of Christ to the world. The Sacrament of the Sick consecrates our suffering and death to the Lord and prepares us further to meet Him face to face.

"You must be born of water and the spirit" John 3:5. The sign with the spirit then effects what is symbolized. In Baptism, the washing away of our sin, and a new life in Christ is effected (i.e., occurs in reality when the water washes our body, and if we have the intent to be Baptized.)

Christ gave us the sacraments as the way to come to Him in a touching relationship.

First, in Baptism, Christ literally "adopts us into His family: He promises to feed us, to heal us, to love us, to give us His name, and offers us an inheritance into all that He is and has!

We even take on His last name, Christian! We can call Him "Abba" or "Father"! We are not just "community" but FAMILY! We are sons and daughters of a living, loving, touching God; nourished and nurtured through His Church, the Body of Christ.

When I was baptized, my name became Frank Dailey Christian. And on judgement day, I can demand my inheritance in His Kingdom, because He promised it, if I have not sold it!

St. Paul tells us in Ephesians 5:5:

"For know this and understand that no fornicator or unclean person, or covetous one, has any inheritance in the kingdom of Christ and God. Let no one lead you astray with empty words."

What St. Paul is saying is that when we commit serious sin, we lose our inheritance, i.e., we take ourselves "out of the family."

If we are out of the family, then we lose all of the privileges of being "in the family," i.e., we can no long call ourselves Christian, we lose our inheritance, we can no longer eat at His family table, which means that we may not receive The Holy Eucharist, or any other "sacrament of the living," until we are again "reconciled" back into the family in THE WAY that Christ has provided – through the

Sacrament of Reconciliation (confession)! The word reconciliation came from the Greek: "con" means "with"; "cilia" is that part of your eye-ball that has color; so what the world implies is that we can again look at this person, in this case, God Himself, eyeball to eyeball!

2) Reconciliation (Confession)

So, if we fall away by serious sin, Christ gave to His apostles the way He wants us to come back to Him again in another touching relationship through His priest in the Sacrament of Reconciliation. On His day of Resurrection (Christ did not wait even one day) He met with His ten apostles (Judas had hanged himself, and they could not find Thomas), He walked through closed doors, and said to them:

"Peace be to you. As the Father has sent Me, I now send you."

When He had said this, He breathed upon them and said to them, "Receive the Holy Spirit, whose sins you forgive, they are forgiven them, whose sins you retain, they are retained." (John 20:19-23).

First, in walking through closed doors Christ showed His divinity, then by showing them His hands and His side, Christ established His humanity and the fact that this was not some "emotional experience," as Satan would have people believe but the actual flesh and blood of the risen Christ.

"He breathed upon them," passing His essence of life into them, and ordained them to act in "His Person" when He said, "as the Father sent me I now send you." He breathe into them the power and authority to teach and do everything that He did including the forgiveness of sins.

All that is in Christ is brought to us by the action of the Holy Spirit (John 14:26; John 16:5-16), so the Holy Spirit acts through them in bringing to us all that is Christ, including the crucified Christ, so that we may personally hand our sins to Christ on the cross, "to be washed in His blood," through that appointed representative of Christ, the priest, in the confessional!

When I go to Confession, I confess my sins; what I am really doing is taking them off, just as when I get home and take off my dirty shirt and hand it to my wife. Because of her love for me she takes my shirt, washes out the dirt, gets it clean again, and returns it to me.

In Confession, I'm taking off my sins and I am handing them to whom?

Some man in the Confession box?

No.!

I am handing them to Christ on the cross who loves me.

When we go to Confession, we are saying, Christ, please take this burden from me. Please wash it in your holy blood which you shed for the love you have for me. (Rev 7:13-15)

He says yes, I will do this, but I ask that you to have sorrow for your sins, and that you try to sin no more.

Then you walk out of Confession cleansed; Christ has taken your burden. You gave it to Him in the way that He asked you to do it through the action of the priest, whom He has ordained to act in His Person. (Persona Christie Cipitis: Art 1948 CCC)

3) The Priesthood (Holy Orders)

Each Priest in the Roman Catholic Church is ordained by a bishop, who was ordained by another bishop, back to one of the twelve apostles. The priesthood has come to us from Christ by apostolic succession, by the apostles handing it on to others. (Acts 1:15-26)

In the Old Testament, God appointed the house of Aaron to be his priest. For almost 2,000 years it was passed on from one generation to another. But the Jews do not have a priesthood anymore? They do not have a priest.

In the year 70 AD, the Romans invaded Jerusalem and killed all the Jewish priests. There was no one to pass on the priesthood. There is no priesthood in the Jewish religion anymore. Only rabbis (teachers).

The priesthood in the Church has to be passed on from one to another back to one of the twelve apostles; the priesthood cannot just start up somewhere, and it is not of the people or from the people, but only by and from Christ (Galatians 1:1), by the action of the Holy Spirit, through the apostleship of Christ.

The early church understood that only those in the apostleship of Christ (the bishops) had the power and authority to pass-on (ordain) others into the priesthood of Christ when they chose Matthias to take the place of Judas (Acts 1:28). Every priest in the Catholic Church can trace his priesthood from a bishop back to another bishop all the way back to one of the twelve apostles (apostolic succession).

St. Paul identifies his priesthood as an "ambassador of Christ . . . Christ coming to us through them" (2 Corinthians 5:18-20). (An ambassador is far more than a representative of an authority; rather, he is "an extension" of that authority and can act in the person of that authority.) St. Paul makes it quite clear that there is only ONE PRIEST, and that is Jesus Christ. Christ then poured His one priesthood out onto His apostles, so that they become an "extension" of that one priesthood; not another priest!

Christ, working through them.

Christ wanted to be a very personal God with a personal touching relationship, and He did this by extending Himself through those He appointed and ordained at the Last Supper, and His day of Resurrection.

John 15:16 clearly shows that Christ appointed His apostles.

"You did not choose me; I chose you and appointed you to go and bear much fruit, the kind of fruit that endures. And so the Father will give you whatever you ask of Him in My name."

And in John 17:18, and John 20:21, "As the Father has sent me, so I send you."

And again at the Last Supper Peter asked, Lord, are you going to leave us? And Christ replied, I have to leave you. If I do not leave you then My spirit cannot come and be with you. What He was saying is that as long as I am here, I am one man; when I go, the Holy Spirit will bring Me to you and then I am not one man, but twelve, and twelve times twelve. You will become an extension of Me, you will act in "My Person.".

Christ was sent to teach, guide and sanctify us. His apostles, through His Church, were commissioned to continue as an extension of Himself to teach, guide and sanctify. Christ did not leave us orphans, and He did not leave us just a book (Bible). His total self continues to be with us in the world for all time IN HIS BODY, THE CHURCH! (Romans 12:5; 1 Corinthians 10:13; Ephesians 4:4-16). So to truly find Christ, we must find the Church He founded, structured and sanctified in truth (John 17:17-23) and which continues in this structure and truth – His Holy Catholic Church.

Christ did not just leave us a book of what He said and did. He left us an authority to interpret and apply His works and actions. Those that believe that He left only a book become their own authority, that is why we have over 25,000 various churches today. Then would we not have as many "churches" as there are people?

4) Holy Eucharist

On the night before He died, after they had eaten the Passover meal, the blessed Lord took bread in His hands and said, "Take and eat, this is My body." Then, He took a cup of wine and said, "Take and drink, this is My blood."

As Catholics, because of what Christ said we believe that that bread literally became His living body. We believe at that moment the cup of wine became the blood of Christ. The bread and wine did not change appearance, but it became the body and the blood of Christ.

Why do we believe this?

Because Christ said it and the church has believed and defended it for 2000 years..

Christ also said, "You must be baptized to be saved."

If we believe in the words of our Lord that something special happens to our soul when we are baptized, is it more difficult to believe His words when He took bread and said, "This is My Body," and the cup of wine and said, "This is My blood"? This sameness of appearance but change of substance we call "Transubstantiation."

We must make sure that Christ really meant what He said. If He really meant what He said, then He would repeat it. We see this in St. John Chapter Six, where the passage goes on for 54 verses. Our blessed Lord had just fed 5,000 men from a few loaves of bread and fishes. Because of this miracle, the crowds want to make Him king. "So he hid himself in the mountains alone." (John 6:15) When evening came his disciples got into a boat and started toward Capharnaum without Jesus. While on the sea a storm arose and they were frightened. "Then Jesus came walking upon the sea and quieted the storm, and immediately the boat was at the land toward which they were going" (John 6:16-21) The next day the crowd got into some boats to follow them.

Question: Why did Christ perform the great miracle of feeding five thousand people with a few loaves and fishes, and then to his apostles follow it up with another great miracle of walking on water and quieting a storm? Was it not because while Christ knew that His apostles had great faith in Him, He knew that they needed a super-human faith in order to accept what He was about to say to them: That He was going to give them His Body to eat and His Blood to drink! Keep in mind also that to drink blood from any animal was a serious sin in the eyes of the Jews.

Remember, the crowd had just seen Him perform a miracle, so they said, "Give us this bread."

Christ said, "The bread I will give you is my body to eat."

Now, that did not sit too well with the people. They responded, "You don't REALLY mean your body to eat."

If Christ meant something else, He would have said, "No, you misunderstood Me. This is not truly My body, but it is just a symbol of My body." This they would have readily accepted, because they had lived with signs and symbols all of their lives.

Instead, He answers their question emphatically in nine different ways. "Unless you eat My body and drink My blood, you shall not have My life in you." (Note: If something is said only once in Scripture, it might be taken figuratively, but if it is repeated three times it is to be taken very literally: here, Christ repeats it three times three – or nine different ways.) Christ even attaches the truth of His ascension to the truth of the Holy Eucharist.

They said, "This is too much," and they left Him, "they walked with Him no more" (John 6:67).

If He had not meant exactly what He said, He would have had to call them back and say, "Wait a minute, you did not understand Me."

Instead, He let them go. The only ones left were the apostles. He said, "Why didn't you go also?"

Peter spoke up and said, "Lord, where would we go? You have the words of eternal life." What Peter is really saying is I honestly do not understand what you are talking about, Lord, but because You have said it, I believe it.

That is faith, i.e., we accept because of His words, not because we understand!

One statement that our Lord makes here in the dissertation on the Holy Eucharist might be confusing – "the flesh profits nothing except with the spirit" (John 6:63).

To understand this statement, it will help to look at what Our Lord said concerning Baptism: "Unless you are born of the water and the spirit, you shall not enter into the kingdom of heaven." Here, Christ is saying that just pouring water over your head will not save you. You must have the intent of being a Christian. The same is true regarding eating His Body – it is of no benefit unless you acknowledge that it IS Christ's Body, and your intent and spirit is to be united to Him in mind and heart AND body in this most perfect way that He has provided.

29

What a great God we have Who has found a way for His own body and blood to come and be in us! Would you want a God who would do any less?

What does the Holy Mass do?

It provides the way for the body and blood of Christ to come and be in us. Through the Holy Eucharist we are children of the body and blood of Christ.

In the Holy Mass, the priest says, "This is my body and this is my blood." We who are Catholics do not understand this miraculous transformation of bread and wine into His body and blood anymore then Peter understood it 2,000 year ago. But because Christ said it was so, we believe it! Not only a symbol, but actually His body and blood. Everything in Christ becomes present-His crucifixion, His resurrection.

Do you see why we kneel at Mass?

We are in the presence of the crucifixion. Not another crucifixion. Christ died one time, two-thousand years ago. But that one time becomes present again every time a Mass is said. If Christ becomes present, the crucifixion becomes present, the resurrection becomes present, here and now (Art 1085, C.C.C), and the body and blood of Christ can actually be in us.

You have to have faith in God Himself. You have to have faith in someone who can create universes to believe such an incredible miracle takes place in the Holy Eucharist. My intelligence convinces me that there is a God; my faith causes me to accept His Word.

And I believe this because of the Word. Anyone who truly believes that the Bible is the Word of God, must believe it.

That is what faith is.

In the early Church, we see in Acts 2:42 that the apostles gathered for prayer, for teachings, and for the communion of the breaking of the bread.

What was just described? The Holy Mass. The word "Mass" comes from the Latin, "Missa," meaning "to send or dismiss." We come to get instruction and receive Christ, and to take Him out into the world as we live our lives. That is what the Mass was 2,000 year ago! This is what the Mass is today.

In Acts 20, verse 7, it tells us that they had begun to meet "on the first day for the breaking of the bread," and hereafter referred to the first day as "the Lord's Day," i.e., His day of resurrection, "the new covenant." There is confusion among some Christians who believe and teach that the emperor Constantine changed the day of worship from the Jewish Sabbath to the first day, that is Sunday the Lord's Day, in 325 AD. This is not the case. The Encyclopedia Britannica, (not a Catholic book) gives this account of Sunday, the Lord's Day "Sunday, first day of the week: in Christianity, the Lord's day, the weekly memorial of Jesus' resurrection for the dead . . . dates back to apostolic times, but details of actual development are not clear, but before the end of the first century, the author of the Book of Revelation gave the first day its name of The Lord's Day (Rev 1:10). St. Justin, martyr in the second century, described Christian worshiping on the "Lord's Day" thusly: the gospels were read, a sermon preached . . . and they celebrated the Lord's supper."

In 1 Corinthians, Chapter 11, St. Paul goes through this last supper. And then he said,

"It follows that if anyone eats the Lord's bread or drinks from his cup in a way that dishonors him, he is guilty of sin against the Lord's body and blood" (1Corinthians 11:27).

St. Paul understood this to be the living body and blood of Christ, and that we must be free of serious sin when we received it! For two thousand years the Catholic Church has taught that this is the living body and blood of Christ.

The "Last Supper" and the "Feast of the Passover" continue in each Mass. Each time you attend Mass, think back 3,500 years to that first Feast of the Passover, and then think back 2,000 years ago to when our Lord was celebrating the Feast of the Passover: YOU ARE THERE; those events become present!

Could our great God do any less for His children? God commanded the Jews to celebrate the Feast of the Passover, and today the Jews still celebrate that feast. This is what our Lord was celebrating and fulfilling. He fulfilled the Feast of the Passover when the blood of the lamb saved the faithful Israelites. His blood, the blood of "the Lamb of God." The New Covenant is our salvation.

At The Last Supper, Christ changed bread and wine into His own Body and Blood so His apostles could have the perfect "blood relationship" with Him. He then commanded His apostles to do this again and again as an extension of Himself so we and all generations may have this perfect "blood relationship with Him." Baptism makes us adopted children of Christ; the Holy Eucharist gives to us

THE WAY to have an even more close and perfect relationship in His family - a blood relationship. COULD OUR LORD AND SAVIOR DO ANY LESS FOR HIS CHILDREN? God does not want to be just "a God out there someplace," but a God who is "with and in us."

5) Matrimony

When a man and woman make a promise to each other to share their lives until death, and to exclude all others in their relationship, we call this agreement "marriage."

When they bring this agreement to be celebrated and sanctified by Christ, then this agreement becomes the Covenant of Matrimony. Once this covenant has been touched by the Person of Christ, it becomes unbreakable by man. Only God, only death of either party frees the other to make another such agreement with another person.

There is no divorce of a validly married man and wife. Such is the dogmatic proclamation by Jesus Christ and accepted by the church from the time of St. Paul to the present day. This is not Church law, it is God's law as given to us by our Lord and Savior Jesus Christ (Mark 10:2-12; Luke 16:18; 1 Corinthians 7:10-11). Any Church claiming Christ's teaching must demand observance of that law of any person who claims to be a member of that Church. If divorce and remarriage are acceptable, then marriage truly becomes just "a piece of paper" as the humanists of the world would have you believe.

6) Annulments

An annulment means an acknowledgement that there was no valid marriage. Failure of either party to declare important information regarding a previous marriage, impotence, no true intent of getting married (such as for political or social reasons only), may in fact be cause for annulment.

If a person is forced into the marriage, is too young or under the influence of drugs which prevent him or her from making a knowledgeable, rational and free-will decision, this may also be a cause for annulment. But, if a valid marriage exists, there is no divorce and remarriage for a Christian, nor can a Christian marry a person who has been divorced (Matthew 5:31-32; 19:3-9; Mark 10:2-12; Luke 16:18; 1 Corinthians 7, 10, 11, 13). Many of the "just causes" in the granting of "civil law" annulments parallel the "just causes" in the granting of "Church law" annulments.

7) Sacrament Of The Sick (Extreme Unction)

St. James, Chapter 15, verses 14-16:

"Is any among you sick? Let him bring in the presbyters (priests) of the Church, and let them pray over him, anointing him with oil (the sign) in the name of the Lord . . .and if he be in sin, they shall be forgiven him. Confess therefore your sins to one another."

Therefore, if we be "in sin", i.e. out of the family of Christ, it is another "way" provided by Christ to again be touched by Him and reconciled back into His loving family as shown in the *Catechism of the Catholic Church.*

"From ancient times in the liturgical traditions of both East and West, we have testimonies to the practice of anointings of the sick with blessed oil. Over the centuries the Anointing of the Sick was conferred more and more exclusively on those at the point of death. Because of this it received the name "Extreme Unction." Notwithstanding this evolution the liturgy has never failed to beg the Lord that the sick person may recover his health if it would be conducive to his salvation. (CCC #1512)

"The special grace of the sacrament of the Anointing of the Sick has as its effects:

- the uniting of the sick person to the passion of Christ, for his own good and that of the whole Church;
- the strengthening, peace, and courage to endure in a Christian manner the sufferings of illness or old age;
- the forgiveness of sins, if the sick person was not able to obtain it through the sacrament of Penance;
- the restoration of health, if it is conducive to the salvation of his soul;
- the preparation for passing over to eternal life." (CCC #1532)

". . . and they cast out many devils, and anointed many sick people with oil and cured them." (Mark 6:13)

5 – THE AUTHORITY OF PETER
AND THE AUTHORITY OF THE POPE

Any organization must have someone in final authority or it will fall apart.

It is true in our country. If we did not have or accept the authority of the President, the country would very soon fall apart. We see revolution after revolution in other countries because they do not accept the final authority of their leader.

The Church needs the same final authority.

Christ knew He must have final authority or else there would be no authority. Many question whether Christ appointed an authority to be an extension of His own authority on this earth. If He did, then we must look to that authority for the interpretation of His Word, the bible.

In this chapter on our Pilgrim's journey, let us look at St. Matthew, Chapter 16, verse 13. Jesus comes into the district of Caesarea Philippi, and He asked His disciples "who do men say the Son of man is?"

Some said John the Baptist, others Elias, others Jeremiah. Jesus listened to these answers, and then asked, "Who do you say I am?"

Imagine, they walked and talked and lived with Jesus for three years, and they still did not know from their experience who He was ("experience" is NOT a substitute or teacher of doctrine. In fact, this ambiguous word today is often being used as an instrument by Satan to cause confusion and dissension to legitimate doctrine and authority.)

Then Peter replied, "Thou art the Christ, the Son of the Living God."

Jesus answered and said,

"Blessed art thou, Simon Bajona (which means the son of John). For flesh and blood hath not revealed it unto thee (no "experience" thing), but my Father in Heaven. And I say to thee, that thou art Peter, and upon this rock I will build my Church; and the gates of hell shall not prevail against it. And I will give unto thee the keys of the kingdom of Heaven; and whatsoever thou shalt bind on earth shall be bound in Heaven and whatsoever thou

shalt loose on Earth shall be loosed in Heaven" (Matthew 16:17-19).

Then He charged His disciples to tell no one that He was Christ, the Son of the Living God.

Let us look at this passage very carefully – it is one of the very important quotations that separate Catholics from non-Catholics. Any person, layman, priest or theologian who does not accept this passage literally is NOT a Catholic!

If we acknowledge the authority of Christ, then this is His authority that He appointed for us to turn to for understanding of what God wants us to believe in, in matters of faith and morals (faith is what we believe; morals are the guidelines of our conduct).

A non-Catholic will say that when Jesus said, "Upon you I will build my Church," that He was talking about a rock that meant faith, not Peter as the rock. Now this would be a good argument except for one thing: What was Peter's name when Christ first met him? Simon, which means, "a reed that bends whichever way the wind may blow."

And what did Jesus do with his name?

He changed it to Peter, which means "rock," a material for a sound foundation, not something that bends with the wind.

God changed the names of His chosen vessels many times.

In the Old Testament, when God first appeared to Abraham, his name was Abram. Abram means "Our father." Then God told Abram that he was pleased with him and would make him the father of "My nation." Then He changed his name to Abraham, which means "The father of many multitudes."

God changed Abram's name to identify his position, the father of the Jewish race.

Who do the Jews say their father is?

Abraham.

Abraham had Isaac, and Isaac had Jacob.

Jacob was so pleasing to God that God made him the seed of "My nation." God told him that his twelve sons would become God's twelve tribes. God then changed his name to Israel, which means "seed."

What do we call Israel's descendants today?

Israelites – the seed of Israel.

God changes Jacob's name to identify his position.

God changes a name many times in the Bible, and each time

He does this, there is a purpose.

So now, Christ comes to Simon and tells him that his name is changed from Simon to rock. Every time the name "rock" is used in the Old Testament, it denotes the presence of God.

When the Jews needed water in the desert, God spoke to Moses, He told him to gather the people together, and it's time for another miracle. And after you have gathered the people together, tell them I've heard their prayers, and when you strike this rock, I shall give you water.

So Moses gathered the people and said that God has heard our prayers, and when I strike the rock we shall have water.

Moses struck the rock and water came out. Not just a stream or a trickle. It had to be a river because they needed water to satiate the thirsts of 100,000 men and their animals.

That river is still there!

Later, when the Jews again needed water, God spoke to Moses. God told them that He had heard his prayer for water. Stand in front of the people, it's time for another miracle. This time instead of striking the rock, God wanted him to speak to the rock.

The rock represented Christ.

And Christ could be struck only once.

So Moses stood in front of the people and said that God has heard our prayers and then something happened that happens to us all so often. We say that I think I know better than God does. It would be more dramatic to strike the rock instead of just speaking to the rock.

And so Moses said, "When I strike the rock we shall have water."

He struck the rock.

Did he get water?

Yes, he did. He had to. Moses was in authority. And if Moses stood up in front of all the people and said, "When I strike the rock we shall have water," and he struck the rock and there was no water, he would have been stoned to death. So God backed up this authority, even though Moses sinned in the way he used it.

Then God told Moses that for this act of disobedience, you shall not be allowed to enter into the Promised Land.

Now, let's go back to Simon.

Christ came to Simon and said, "I am the rock . . . I am the cornerstone."

Then, He turned to Peter and said, "You are the rock."

What is He doing?

He is appointing Peter to "act in His Person" as head of His Church on earth.

We find that after His resurrection, in John 21:15, Christ was with His apostles again. And He asked, "Peter, do you love Me."

Peter replied, "Christ, you know I love Your."

He said, "Feed My lambs."

He asked again, "Peter, do you love Me?"

Peter said, "lord, you know I love You."

He said, "Feed My lambs."

Then, a third time, He asked, "Peter, do you love Me?"

Christ said, "Feed My sheep."

In this one Scripture, Christ said to Peter to "feed My lambs," meaning baby lambs, "feed My labs," meaning the older lambs, and "feed My sheep," the oldest of the sheep.

At that moment, what authority was given to Peter?

Christ made him the shepherd of His flock, in charge of the laymen, the priests and the bishops!

Who does Christ say that He is?

The Good Shepherd, and there shall be "one fold and one shepherd" (John 10:17).

He is transferring this title and this commission to Peter!

And then He said, "Peter, whatsoever you bind on earth, I will bind in Heaven. Whatsoever you loose on Earth, I will loose in Heaven."

Christ is saying that the decisions you make here on earth, Peter, I will verify in heaven. If you bind a decision there, I will bind it here. If you loose them, I will loose them.

Who is speaking?

Jesus Christ is speaking.

To whom is He speaking?

The one man, Peter.

So Christ established His Church on the authority of Peter.

Remember, He gave to Peter the keys to the Kingdom of Heaven.

You have the keys to your house, even if the bank owns it. You have the keys. If someone wants to enter your locked house, they have to come to you and do what you deem is necessary to get into the house. You will tell them what is necessary, what the conditions are.

When you go to a movie theater, the man who has the keys tells you what is necessary to get in, i.e. that it will cost you five or six dollars. He does not own the building or the movie, but he has the keys so he has the authority to do this.

Peter has the keys to the Kingdom of Heaven.

And so, if Peter has the keys, he has the God-given authority to say what is necessary to get into the Kingdom of God.

He has the keys.

So this authority tells us what we must believe, matters of faith, and what we must do, what must be our conduct with each other and with our bodies, matters of morals.

The authority of Peter tells us what is necessary to get into the Kingdom of Heaven. He does not own heaven, but he does have the keys.

Christ said, "Whatever thou shalt bound on earth shall be bound in Heaven, whatever shall be loosed on earth, shall be loosed in Heaven."

Christ said that the decisions you make here are the decisions I will ratify in Heaven.

God has assured us that when this earthly authority speaks; it is Christ speaking through this authority. By the promise of Christ he will not let us go astray.

There are many examples in the early days of the Church where Peter exercises his authority.

First of all, as we go through the scriptures, notice that almost every time it mentions "the apostles" it reads "Peter and the apostles." There can be no doubt whatsoever that Peter was the one in authority.

Let us take a look at one of the first places where this authority was exercised.

This is in Acts, Chapter 15. There was a discussion in the Church as to whether or not they should continue to circumcise. The dissension on this matter was ready to split the Church wide open. Half of the believers said, "Yes, we must continue because circumcision was commanded by Moses." Circumcision was as important to the Jews as Baptism is to us. The other half of the believers said "No"; a decision had to be made on this matter so they brought it to Peter.

The apostles and the presbyters held a meeting to look into the matter. After a long debate, Peter got up and said to them,

"Brethren you know that in the early days, God made choice among us so that through my mouth the Gentiles shall hear the word of the gospel and believe. And God who knows the heart bore witness by giving them the Holy Spirit just as he did to us and they made no distinction between us and them, but cleansed their heart by faith. Why then, do you now try to test God by putting on the neck of the disciples, the yolk that neither our fathers nor we have been able to bear but we are saved through the grace of our Lord Jesus just as they were." (Acts 15:7-11)

Peter gathered them together and listened to the discussion. And, after the discussion, he stood up and he said I remind you Christ appointed me. By my mouth shall come the word that they may believe and I therefore say we no longer have to circumcise.

Once he made this proclamation, the meeting quieted down. We see later in Acts, Chapter 15, verse 28, St. James writes of this decision to all of the Churches.

"For the Holy Spirit and we have decided to lay no further burden upon you but this indispensable one to abstain from things sacrificed to idols, blood and what is strangled and from immorality."

St. James is saying the "Holy Spirit and we have made this decision." He understood that the Holy Spirit was working through them for this decision.

At the end of the chapter, St. Paul writes, "1 command them to keep the precepts of the apostles and the presbyters in Jerusalem."

As we go on into Acts, Chapter Sixteen, verse 4, St. Paul says,

"As they passed through the cities they delivered to the brethren for their observance the decision arrived at by the apostles and the presbyters in Jerusalem."

St. Paul had a question about circumcision, and he acted as any proper theologian should when he has a question — he brought it to the men in authority. Once the decision was made by St. Peter, then the Catholic theologian does as St. Paul did. He accepts it in faith as coming from Christ by the action of the Holy Spirit, and now explains the decision made by the men in authority, in light of scripture and tradition.

And from then on in the Bible, you see St. Paul explaining this decision and condemning anyone whom does not accept it.

40

As we go into Galatians, Chapters One and Two, St. Paul first identifies his position in the Church in verse one:

"Paul, an apostle sent not from men nor by man but by Jesus Christ and God the Father." (i.e., the power of the priesthood does not come from "community" but by and from Jesus Christ and the Father!)

Then, he goes on to say, as we go into verse six,

"I marvel then that you are so quickly deserting him who called you to the grace of Christ changing to another gospel, which is not another gospel except in this respect, except there are some that trouble you and wish you to pervert the gospel of Christ."

If you get upset about the heresies in the Church today (a heresy is a false teaching), do not be too upset because it happened in St. Paul's time. Many heresies came up, and they had to put them down.

St. Paul goes on to say,

"Even if an angel from Heaven should preach a Gospel to you other than that what we (the Church) have preached to you, let him be anathema." (If St. Paul were alive today in the Church, he might add after the word "angel" or "dissident theologian.")

That's about the strongest word he could use without truly swearing; it means, "let him be a Satan."

And again, he repeats himself.

"Anyone preaching gospel to you other than that which you have received, let him be anathema. They are seeking the favor of men not of God."

Now, an interesting thing develops as we go further in this passage.

St. Paul says, "I did not receive the teaching of Christ from any man, but I received it by the revelation of Jesus Christ."

St. Paul was not taught by any man. All of his knowledge of Christ was by Divine Revelation. But then St. Paul goes on and tells us in the next chapter,

"I went up in consequence of a revelation and conferred with them on the Gospel which I preach among the gentiles, but separately with the men of authority, thus perhaps I should be running or run in vain."

St. Paul says I went to the men of authority to verify that my teaching was proper.

41

St. Paul had his knowledge by Divine Revelation and yet he still went to the men of authority to verify that his teaching was proper.

And, in verse six of Chapter Two, he says,

"But from the men of authority what they once were matters not to me, God accepts not the person or the man, the men of authority lay no further burden upon me."

Paul was talking about circumcision in this particular instance. Paul says that the men in authority said we no longer have to circumcise.

Now, we know that Paul and Peter did not get along very well. Paul was a highly educated man, and Peter was a fisherman. Yet highly educated Paul must now take orders from the fisherman. That must have galled him a little bit, so he mentions here "it matters not to me what they once were, God accepts not the person or the man."

St. Paul is saying that it doesn't matter that Peter is just an old fisherman, he was the one appointed by God and I accept his authority.

Now, when you show or read this passage to a non-Catholic, he or she will probably refer you to verse eleven in this same chapter, so let us take a look at it.

"But when Peter came to Antioch, I withstood him to his face, because he was deserving of blame. For before that certain persons came from James, he used to eat with the Gentiles, but when they came he began to withdraw and separate himself from the circumcised. And the rest of the Jews disassembled along with them so that Barnabas also was led away with them into this dissimulation."

What needs to be clarified here is precisely what St. Paul is standing up to St. Peter about. Peter had begun to separate himself from the Gentiles, so Paul said that he stood up to him and told him this was not proper. This is not the Christian thing to do. You're not supposed to separate yourself.

This issue had nothing to do with challenging the authority of Peter on faith and morals. It is Paul correcting the personal conduct of Peter, which we can do with the Pope himself. It was about personal conduct.

So, in no way does this passage lessen Paul's acceptance of

Peter's authority.

Now, all non-Catholic Christians have a little problem here (especially those who are adamant about Old Testament food and the Sabbath): circumcision was demanded in the Old Law. It was their baptism so to speak, and Christ was circumcised. Christ did not say that we do not have to be circumcised.Either we must continue to circumcise according to the Law of Moses, or we must accept that Peter had the authority to "loose" the Christian of that obligation. There is no third choice if we really are going to adhere to the new covenant. Once Peter "stood up" and made that decision, the discussion was over!

As we go through the history of the Church, every time a serious decision has to be made, it is made in the same way as it was made in Jerusalem. The successors of the apostles, those who have received their authority from those before them, the bishops, gather together. They have a great deal of discussion. After the discussion, the Pope, who now succeeds Peter, stands up and says, 'I remind you that Christ chose me. I am acting in the continuation of Peter that through my mouth shall come the word to the Gentiles that they may believe.'

Then he may make a proclamation of faith and morals the same as Peter did.

This has already happened a number of times throughout the history of the Church.

In the fourth century, there arose the heresy of Arianism where they were denying that Christ was truly God. They said, Well, He is sort of a God, but He is not equal to God the Father and God the Holy Spirit. He is sort of a second-rate God.'

That was the heresy of Arianism. It has been reborn again in our present day in at least one sect, the Jehovah Witness sees God as only one person.

And so, in 325 AD the Church called a council at Nicaea. At this council Pope Sylvester I proclaimed that he had listened to all the discussions, and he then proclaimed that Christ is God, equal to God the Father and God the Holy Spirit in all things, therefore, three person, not one; yet exist as One God.

From that council, and in the next two councils that followed, came the profession of faith that Catholics profess together at every Mass. That profession of faith, called the Nicene Creed, has been our Proclamation of Faith to the present day. This precedent goes back to Peter, of clarifying a truth.

Whenever there was a question about faith or morals, Peter made the decision. When all of the bishops together with Peter (or his successor, the Pope), make a decision, it is said to be "infallible." They cannot err on matters of faith and morals, not because of themselves, but because of the promise of Christ that the Holy Spirit would enlighten them, and bring to them all that is Christ. (John 14:26; John 16:5-16)

Christ said, "What you bind on earth I will bind in heaven, what you loose on earth I will loose in heaven." This has been the consistent teaching of the Church for two thousand years, and we have faith that God will protect this authority, and He has protected it! For over 2,000 years this authority has never changed any doctrine of the Church, or any words of the Bible.

And it never will.

We have had Popes who have been bad Popes, who have been sinful Popes; there are probably some Popes who are in Hell right now. But never in those 2,000 years has God ever allowed His doctrine to be changed. He has protected His teaching through the Church. He has been true to His word.

If anyone can show me a doctrine that has been changed in these 2,000 years, I would question whether the Catholic Church is the true faith. There are only changes of certain understandings, and, at times, there are changes in the applications.

If you see a man one block away, you can clearly determine that it is a human being (in my day, you could even tell if it was a man or a woman). As you get closer to this person, you can begin to see details - the color of their hair, their eyes, the contours of their face.

The same process is true in what we call the development of doctrine or the understanding of doctrine. There can be no doctrinal changes, but there can be development through time as we have a more complete understanding of the issues.

There has been no new doctrine in the Catholic Church since the Apostolic Age, nor will there ever be!

None can be changed, none can be added, none can be taken away. Putting it very simply, the Pope and the Church are NOT above the Bible or the Apostolic Tradition, which we call 'the Deposit of Faith.' But, rather, they are both servants to it! The purpose of Church authority is to explain and apply what is there. But, there are certain kinds of developments that might alter an application. Let me give you a very simple example.

In the old days, before they had monetary exchanges, it was not unusual for a man to loan you money and charge you a 100% interest for one month or for a year. This is called "usury." The Church said that this was not fair and 'since there is no way we can control the interest you charge, you cannot loan money and charge interest.'

You could not loan money and charge interest because of these abuses.

But, as time went on, and society began to get control of this problem by passing laws, and the interest rates became more reasonable and controllable, the Church said, 'Okay, the abuse now is gone, therefore you can loan money and charge interest if it is a reasonable interest.'

The law had not changed. The application of the law had changed. The law is, 'You may not use your own money to abuse someone else.'

That is the law.

The application can and does change, but the law itself can never change.

What is the Official Post Vatican II Teaching in the Church in regards to the Pope?

It is strongly urged that all Catholics to get a copy of the Catechism of the Catholic Church (CCC) to use in identifying what IS Catholic teaching and in correcting heretical teachings in their own parish or diocese. Copies may be obtained from any Catholic bookstore or by ordering from: United States Catholic Conference, 1312 Massachusetts Avenue, NW, Washington, D.C. 20005.)

St. John reminds us,

"Anyone who comes to you and does not abide in the doctrine of Christ (i.e. His Church) has not God . . . do not receive him . . . whoever says to him welcome, shares in the evil that he does." (2 John 8-11)

Every Catholic has an obligation to learn what IS church teaching, and to defend it, even if the erroneous teaching were by a priest or a bishop. The CCC gives you a powerful tool to do this. Do expect to be put down and embarrassed by those who have expertise, and do expect to be called Pre-Vatican II." But, the CCC was composed Post Vatican II.

This Council of Vatican II, as in all of the other twenty-one councils, did NOT change what the Church IS, i.e., "The Body of Christ, with Christ as the 'invisible head'," working by the action of the Holy Spirit, through the "visible head," the successor of Peter. And, no council ever changes what the Church DOES, i.e., bringing us the teaching, authority and sanctification of Christ. As some of the other councils did, Vatican II clarified certain truths and doctrines, and changed some of "the ways" of doing things. A council can change "the way" of doing things, such as the way of saying Mass or hearing confessions; no council can change "what" the Church does.

Here are some excerpts from some of the vital articles contained in the CCC. Those comments not in quotation marks are my own.

"The CCC, which I approved June 25th last and the publication of which I today order by virtue of my Apostolic Authority, is a statement of the Church's faith and of catholic doctrine, attested to or illumined by Sacred Scripture, the Apostolic Tradition, and the Church's Magisterium. I declare it to be a sure norm for teaching the faith and thus a valid and legitimate instrument for ecclesial communion. May it serve the renewal to which the Holy Spirit ceaselessly calls the Church of God, the Body of Christ, on her pilgrimage to the undiminished light of the Kingdom!" (CCC page 5 #3 1st paragraph)

"Moved by the grace of the Holy Spirit and drawn by the Father, we believe in Jesus and confess: "You are the Christ, the Son of the living God." On the rock of this faith confessed by St. Peter, Christ built His Church." (CCC #424).

"When Christ instituted the Twelve, "he constituted [them] in the form of a college or permanent assembly, at the head of which he placed Peter, chosen from among them." Just as "by the Lord's institution, St. Peter and the rest of the apostles constitute a single apostolic college, so in like fashion the Roman Pontiff, Peter's successor, and the bishops, the successors of the apostles, are related with and united to one another." (CCC # 880).

"The Lord made Simon alone, whom he named Peter, the "rock" of his Church. He gave him the keys of his Church and instituted him shepherd of the whole flock. "The office of binding and loosing which was given to Peter was also assigned to the college of apostles united to its head." This pastoral office of Peter and the

46

other apostles belongs to the Church's very foundation and is continued by the bishops under the primacy of the Pope." (CCC #881)

"The Pope, Bishop of Rome and Peter's successor, "is the perpetual and visible source and foundation of the unity both of the bishops and of the whole company of the faithful." "For the Roman Pontiff, by reason of his office as Vicar of Christ, and as pastor of the entire Church has full, supreme, and universal power over the whole Church, a power which he can always exercise unhindered." (CCC #882)

"The college or body of bishops has no autho9rity unless united with the Roman Pontiff, Peter's successor, as its head." As such, this college has "supreme and full authority over the universal Church; but this power cannot be exercised without the agreement of the Roman Pontiff." (CCC #883)

The Pope does not have to consult with any part of the Church to make these decisions. He makes them on his own. And they, of themselves, are correctly called irreformable.

'Even when he is not speaking ex-cathedra (which is when he stands up and proclaims himself as a successor of Peter and makes a proclamation), his teachings on matters of faith and morals demand religious submission of will and of mind.'

Some maintain that "We only have to accept the Pope's infallible proclamations."

That is not true.

We must also accept his authoritative teachings. The infallible proclamations are usually made on matters of faith, or to define a truth, as in the case of the Arian heresy. When the Pope said, "Christ is God, equal to God the Father and God the Holy Spirit in all things," he was defining a truth.

That is a matter of faith.

Morals have to do with our conduct.

In matters of morals, the Pope gives authoritative teaching. For example, when he repeats something again and again, consistently, then it becomes authoritative teaching. It is usually not a declared "ex-Cathedra" teaching, as are the matters of faith.

"Ex-Cathedra" declarations are "set in concrete," so to speak; once they are made, they can never, be changed, because they define a truth. Authoritative teaching, which usually involves the interpretation and application of a moral law, may change, as noted in the matter of charging interests on money loaned.

That is why the Pope generally does not make "ex-Cathedra" teachings on matters of morals (though he may do so).

As Catholics, we accept that the Pope's authority was conferred by Christ, and by the promise of Christ will bring us what is the will of Christ.

We who are Catholic believe that Jesus Christ is the Invisible Head of our Church, and He now works through the visible head, who today is the Pope. The Pope exists as the visible head to bring us His teaching, His authority and His sanctification, so that we can come to Christ.

When the Pope speaks, he speaks with the authority of Christ when he speaks on matters of faith and morals.

If the Pope talks about politics or science, etc., you can say, 'That's nice, but I'm not interested.' (One Pope even said that the world was flat, not round; he was NOT infallible when speaking about science.) But when he speaks on matters of faith and morals, we must consent with our will and our mind.

Today, there are certain theologians and their followers who feel that they can legitimately disagree with certain teachings of the church, especially on sexual morality. Their reasoning, according to one theologian, is: ". . .The Church is the Body of Christ and we ARE the Church, therefore what comes from 'us' is coming from the 'Body of Christ,' and therefore is of and from Christ Himself. Therefore, it is the 'experience of the faith community' that should be making these decisions on abortion, birth control, divorce and remarriage, etc., not some man in Rome."

Now, there are people who have read books written by men of human wisdom. They have credentials to testify to their expertise in theology, but, they have become quite confused because they have forgotten or ignore a very simple fact of anatomy: every living and functioning body must have a head, and it is the head that has authority over all members of that body. While the body may have multiple fingers and toes, arms and legs, it has only ONE head!

Any part of the body that refuses to accept that authority must be cut off "and cast outside — cast into fire, and they shall burn" (John 15:1-7).

We who are Catholics acknowledge that Jesus Christ is the Invisible Head of this one Church that He founded, structured and sanctified; and that, by the action of the Holy Spirit, He works through the visible head that He appointed, Peter and his successors.

The decisions by this 'successor of Peter' on 'faith and morals' are not coming from 'some man in Rome,' but are coming through him from Jesus Christ. If we reject what comes from this authority, then we are rejecting the authority itself and the one who appointed the authority, Jesus Christ! (NOTE: I deeply respect any person who after intelligent and objective evaluation does not accept this doctrine of Papal Authority, and so identifies himself as a non-Catholic. However, anyone who does not accept the fullness of the Pope's authority, and yet calls himself a 'Catholic,' is either confused or a liar, leading others into confusion or toward Satan. Confusion is the single most effective weapon that Satan has in causing intellectual and spiritual loss of faith.)

Theologians certainly have a right and an obligation to bring questions to this authority, as they did to Peter in regard to the question of circumcision. But once they have been given the answer, then they must accept that answer or decision "by the men of authority", as did St. Paul.

I repeat, if they reject what comes from an authority then, in fact, they have rejected the authority itself and so should identify themselves as non-Catholic. Further dissension and discussion only serve to divide and confuse the faithful and have no useful purpose except to give notoriety and publicity for those doing the dissenting. When the Pope visited the United States in 1989, he spoke to our bishops clearly and decisively in regard to dissenting theologians. The following are his direct quotes:

"To accept faith is to give assent to the Word of God as transmitted by the Church's authentic Magisterium."

"Dissent from Church doctrine remains what it is, dissent; as such it may not be proposed or received on an equal footing with the Church's authentic teaching."

"It is sometimes claimed that dissent from the Magisterium is totally compatible with being a "good Catholic" and poses no obstacle to the reception of the sacraments. This is a grave error that challenges the teaching office of the bishops of the United States and elsewhere."

Question: Why have our bishops not acted more aggressively in identifying these dissenters and correcting their teachings? Why do they allow them to speak in their diocese, and even be paid to lecture and direct certain catechetical conferences and Catholic institutions and schools? We, the laity, deserve an explanation!

God will demand an explanation!

The Church is a 'mystery,' i.e., no one can fully understand all that it is. However, in Holy Scripture, St. Paul gives us an excellent place to start: "THE CHURCH IS THE BODY OF CHRIST" (I Cor. 12, 27-31); (Vatican II, The Church, Article 14). Everything that is YOU is in your body: your heart, your mind, your spirit, your soul, and YOUR person.

If the Church is indeed "The Body of Christ," then the complete Christ comes to us only in and through the one Church. He founded, directed and sanctified it to be a continuation of Himself in the world until the end of time!

The function of a "body" is to take a "person" where he wants to go so that he can do what he wants to do. WHERE CHRIST WANTS TO GO IS TO YOU, AND WHAT HE WANTS TO DO WHEN HE GETS THERE IS TO GIVE TO YOU ALL THAT IS NECESSARY FOR YOUR SALVATION!

Clearly and with certainty, He wishes to TEACH the TRUTHS about God and His Kingdom (matters of faith).

And TEACH the GUIDELINES or LAWS that we must follow in our conduct in this life (matters of morals).

He wishes to provide us with definitive LEADERSHIP and ENLIGHTENMENT so that we will not be confused or led astray.

He wishes to cleanse us of our sins and SANCTIFY us (make us worthy to be called Children of God).

He wishes to be "with us" and "IN us" in a very special, personal way.

He wishes to unite us to Him as Loving Father and to each other as brothers and sisters.

He wishes that by our words and actions we give witness and testimony of Him to the world, i.e., that we LIVE in Christ, and that He lives in us.

The Church, then, being the Body of Christ, must bring to us the Person of Christ, the Teaching of Christ, the Authority of Christ, and the Sanctification of Christ; the Church must give witness and testimony to the world.

Jesus Christ founded and structured His Church so that it would do just that. St. Paul goes on to say that we are all 'members of this body' and each member is important for the whole body to function properly in its mission. No member or group is more or less important than the other, nor can one preempt or replace the other (1 Cor.

12, 12-31); (Vatican II, The Church, Article 13).

Christ structured this body so that it is made up of members who "rule" in the authority of Christ (Pope and hierarchy); members who "teach in the name of Christ" (the bishops, *when teaching in unison with the Pope and the Magisterium*); members who sanctify in the Person of Christ (priesthood); and members who give witness and testify and LIVE Christ (the laity).

All and together we ARE "The People of God;" or, a much better terminology which is laced all through the Old and New Testament, THE FAMILY OF GOD.

The community, or family, is why the Church exists. But we must always remember that 'of itself' this 'Community' has no authority to govern, no power of the priesthood to sanctify, and no commission to teach except that which is given to it by Christ Himself through Peter and the Apostles. Pope John Paul II reminds us, "It is Christ alone who teaches . . .who governs . . . who sanctifies...transmitted through the Church" (Apostolic Exhortation on Catechetics, October 25, 1979).

The "Person of Christ" is brought to us through His Priesthood. The "Presence and Sanctification of Christ" exists in and through His Sacraments. The "Teaching of Christ" rests in and is guarded by the Magisterium of the Church. The "Authority of Christ" was given to St. Peter and his successors. That part of the Church, which gives witness and testifies of Christ, is the laity.

As a Doctor of Medicine, let me offer my own anatomical, physiological composition of the Church as the Body of Christ, and of we laity being part of that Body:

The laity are the arms and legs, fingers and toes that take the body where it wants to go and helps it do what it needs to do.

But to remain alive and part of the body, it is necessary for them to have a blood supply to bring nutrition and oxygen. The blood supply is the sacraments that give us nourishment and life.

The blood must be supplied by the heart. The heart is the priesthood that brings us the sacraments of life and nourishment.

The members do not move without intervention to stimulate the muscles. That intervention is for the social good, and comes from our bishops, who, although they are a separate entity from the brain, are nevertheless totally dependent on the brain so there will be a coordinated and progressive movement of the members.

The anatomical brain is the Papacy, the successor of Peter.

The will, and ultimate authority of this brain — the spirit of this brain — is Jesus Christ.

Before Christ, only the Jewish religion contained God's promise. Christ came to fulfill those promises, not to destroy them (Matthew 5: 17-20). Christ brought this fullness of truth and salvation in a new and everlasting covenant to this one religion and sanctified it in His blood. There really can be only one truth of God and from God: there can be only one Church and that IS the Catholic Church, the fullness of Christ.

The Church is the "Body of Christ" and where the living body IS, the Person IS; therefore, to find the fullness of Christ, the TOTAL CHRIST, we MUST find and accept His Church. We must all diligently search for that Church that Christ founded and structured and sanctified to bring us a continuation of Himself to all generations. That Church must continue in His authority, His Priesthood and Sacraments, and His teaching.
Should you accept any less than His Catholic Church?

". . . glory be to him from generation to generation in the Church and in Christ Jesus for ever and ever. Amen." (Ephesians 3:21)

"Conscience" comes from the Latin: "con" meaning "with", and "scire" meaning "to know"; hence, a judgment formed with knowledge.

Conscience is your judgment of what is right and wrong in relation to a set of laws. You have a conscience in regards to civil laws. You read the laws and you form what is right and wrong in relation to that law, as interpreted and applied by our courts and judges, especially the Supreme Court of our country.

You have a social conscience, i.e., issues of personal hygiene. And you have a religious conscience.

Your religious conscience has to be formed by and with the knowledge of God's law — by revelation from God, or from understanding through His. God gave us revelation so that we could have an informed conscience. We must form our conscience as to what is God's law, and then make our judgment from that point. (CCC #1785)

Here is one critical question you have to ask yourself: 'If God told you to do something that you felt violated your conscience, would you do it?' Sure you would, if you were absolutely sure it was God speaking. You would correct your conscience. We who are believers must form our conscience to coincide with the laws of

God.

Those who are not believers try to change the laws of God to coincide with their conscience. The abortionists do this. That is the difference between a true Christian and one who wants to play at being a Christian. When you find out what is God's law, you must change to conform to His laws. Do not try to change His laws to conform to what you feel, or the experience of community. "Am I trying to please God or man?" (Galatians 1: 9-10).

Many 'experiences' result in heresies that develop from time to time. Going by "experience alone" reduces the Bible and Church teaching to a 'human experience thing,' negated or changeable by further 'human experiences,' resulting in the formation of 'Humanism' or 'Modernism' or 'Spiritual Liberalism,' or 'Jungism,' or 'Radical Feminism' which is the Church of Satan. For example, many today say we must accept pluralism in the Church. Well, that depends upon how you define it. (Pluralism means that there are two sets of teachings.) Now, if you mean by "pluralism" that you should accept different ways of saying the same thing, yes, we should accept that. It is no different than calling our President 'the Chief Executive of the United States,' or 'the President of the United States.'

If there is a pluralism that gives you two different doctrines, we cannot accept that. This type of accepting different doctrines and calling it 'acceptable pluralism' is the cliche or slogan used by those who wish to cause confusion, and the destruction of the Church. "Do not be led away by empty words and slogans." (1 Timothy 3:13; 6:35; 2 John 3:11; 1 Corinthians 2:19, etc.).

So pluralism must always be true to doctrine as it is outlined in the official Church documents if it is to be accepted.

Perhaps in all of scripture, that which is most misinterpreted is in St. John, Chapters 13, 14, 15, 16 & 17 when Jesus promises to send the Holy Spirit "Who will teach you all things . . ." A person reading this will assume that it applies to himself personally. When Jesus says something, the person to whom he says it is as important as are the words. On the mountain speaking to the multitudes He said 'you may not change anything,' but speaking to one man, Peter, He said, "whatever you bind (change) on I will bind in heaven; whatever you loose on earth (change) I will loose in heaven" (Matt. 16,19). At the Last Supper He was speaking only to His Twelve Apostles and in effect saying when you twelve, with Peter as the one in authority, gather as leaders of my Church then "the Holy Spirit will guide you in all things." On an individual basis, even the Apostles were confused about circumcision. Only when they gathered, as church with Peter in authority was the question clarified (Acts 15, 15-20).

6 – MARY IN THE CHURCH

Mary cannot save your soul; you can be saved only through Jesus Christ. Her mission in the Church is to help lead us to Christ.

Many of the most beautiful dissertations on the Blessed Virgin Mary have come from Archbishop Fulton J. Sheen. Therefore, a great deal of these words, thoughts and inspirations will have come from him. Archbishop Sheen has written that God might very well have two pictures of us: one is what we are, and the other is what we might be. In all of creation, the only person who could possibly be chosen to be the Mother of Christ would be that singular person whose picture in God's mind of what she could be was exactly the same as the picture of what she was.

Mary is not a goddess and has no power or authority of her own other than that given her by and through God. Our power of reasoning must conclude that Mary, chosen to be the earthly mother of "the Son of God," has to be the most perfect, and therefore, the most honored, of all of God's creatures.

Catholic understanding about the Virgin Mary, mother of Jesus, is based in part on the place the Second Vatican Council gave to Mary. The key statements are found in the "Constitution on the Sacred Liturgy" and in the final chapter of the "Dogmatic Constitution on the Church."

The Gospel offers a comparison between Abraham and Mary. God was so pleased with Abraham that He willed that His chosen people would come from his (Abraham's) seed. To this day, the Jews honor him by calling him "Abraham, our father." Likewise, because Mary was so pleasing to God, He chose her to be the mother of the one who would be the salvation of mankind. She is thus honored by us by being called, "Mary, our Mother." The unique honor given to her in Holy Scripture is that "all generations shall call me Blessed." (Luke 1:48)

As truth, grace, authority and sanctification comes from Christ through the apostles and their successors, i.e., the bishops and their priests (John 20: 21-23), this hierarchy then is representative of that which is Christ. Mary, being a recipient of this truth, grace and sanctification, symbolizes 'the community of the Church,' i.e., we the people.

Tradition tells us that the reason Mary remained here on earth after the Ascension of Christ was to be an inspiration and example to us of what a 'member of the Mystical Body of Christ' should be. Mary, then, is truly the patron saint of the people of the Body of Christ the Church.

John's gospel pictures Mary at Cana and at Calvary - beginning and the end of her son's public life. About Mary's later life, the Scriptures are silent. The last time she appears is in the Acts of the Apostles, at the heart of the band of apostles praying for the coming of the Holy Spirit at Pentecost.

The Immaculate Conception (Mary's freedom from original sin) and the Assumption (Mary's being one with the risen Christ in the fullness of her being: body, as well as soul) — both doctrines have been solemnly proclaimed as revealed truth in dogmatic definitions by Pope Plus IX in 1864, and by Plus XII in 1950. Mary's last statement in Holy Scripture describes well her mission and purpose (John 2:5): *"Jesus' mother then told the servants, 'Do whatever he tells you'."* Basically, her message at Fatima was exactly the same message, telling us to do all that Christ has commanded us to do.

Our ultimate salvation can be accomplished only by the sacrifice made by another: our Lord and Savior Jesus Christ. Therefore, it follows that if we offer to God our own prayers and sacrifices for another; He must accept this in their name. Mary's perfection of spirit must include a perfection of love.

Her "perfect love" assures each of us that she loves us as her own children. If we ask Mary and the saints to plead our case before God, then will not they respond and will God not listen?

How could Christ refuse His own most perfect creation, His own mother and those who have served Him well? Therefore, we ask Mary and the saints to pray for us in exactly the same way that we ask a priest or minister or friend to pray for us. This is not in place of prayer to God, but is in addition to prayer. That Christ answers Mary's prayer is proved by the many miraculous cures of the sick at Fatima, Lourdes, and other shrines that honor her throughout the world. These miracles are documented and proved by definitive medical tests and authorities so as to remove any possibility of emotionalism or uncertainty.

7 – PURGATORY

Stating it very simply, purgatory is the state of cleansing before we are admitted to our heavenly kingdom. Perhaps we might better understand it if we evaluate some rather obvious facts: A soul would merit hell only for a serious, un-repented offense against Almighty God (a mortal sin). Yet, man cannot enter Heaven with any stain of sin on his soul, ". . . nothing profane shall enter heaven . . ." (Rev 21:27). Therefore, what is to happen to a man who has a small (venial) sin on his soul for which he has not yet repented?

God in His justice would certainly not condemn him to hell, and yet only those whose 'robes are washed white' may enter into the kingdom of Heaven. There must be a way and a place of cleansing. The Church calls this place purgatory. We may debate the time and the type of suffering that we may expect because of our own voluntary offenses against God and our fellowman. Make no mistake about it, God has been very definitive through revelation in the Old and New Testaments that we must expect punishment for our sins. The Church teaches that the suffering of purgatory will be a punishment, but only for a limited time. How long and how much no one really knows, but she relates it to us in relative terms which we can comprehend.

Old and New Testaments indicate repeatedly that there are good works and prayers that will lessen the punishment due us because of our sins (St. James 5:19-20). Prayers and acts which acknowledge God and those who have served Him well certainly are pleasing to Him, and such devotion we believe will lessen the punishment which we deserve. The Church calls these indulgences and relates such prayers or acts in relative terms as days of indulgences. Certain great acts of faith, penance or charity, the Church teaches, may result in a plenary indulgence, which is the removal of all punishment due for all sins of the past.

Christ and the Magisterium of the Church have always taught that the merit of a gift or act has no relationship to the amount of the gift or the greatness of the act itself, but rather by the intent and sacrifice involved. Christ made this very clear in His story about the "widow's mite."

Scriptural Basis for Purgatory and Prayers for the Dead:

The fact is well established in the Old and New Testaments that there is forgiveness of sin and yet also there remains punishment due because of our sin. Forgiveness basically means that God has accepted us back into His family and we can again eat at His table and re-establish our inheritance to His kingdom.

Forgiveness does not necessarily mean TOTAL remission of punishment. God forgave the Jews for adoring the golden calf because of the intercession of Moses on their behalf (Exodus 32:10-14). "And the Lord was appeased from doing the evil which He has spoke against His people," and yet for this and many transgressions, they also received punishment of atonement for sins. Moses was forgiven for his transgression but as punishment he was not allowed to enter into the Promised Land (Numbers 20:8-13). There are also instances of God accepting prayer and sacrifices of others as appeasement; i.e., Numbers 14. But even here, the people were punished by not being allowed to enter the Promised Land. Jesus repeatedly stated that man would be punished for his sins. So what of the sins for which man has not been punished but for which he has been forgiven?

Again, God in His love cleanses our soul in justice; this we call purgatory. But how can our prayers help those who have gone on before us? Logical thinking tells us if we offer prayer or sacrifice on behalf of another, living or dead, God would so accept it. The biblical basis for this thinking is as follows:

"It is therefore a holy and wholesome thought o pray for the dead, that they might be loosed from their sins" (2 Maccabees 12:43-40).

"Jesus said, 'Come to terms quickly with thy opponent while thou art on the way within this life, lest thy opponent deliver thee to the judge (God), and the judge to the officer (Satan) and thou be cast into prison (hell or suffering). Amen, I say to thee, thou will not come out of it (place of cleansing – "purgatory" we call it) until thou hast paid the last penny" (Matthew 5:25-26)

Luke 12:58-59 contains basically the same statement as Matthew 5:25-26.

"Jesus said, 'Whoever speaks against the Holy Spirit (ascribe to the devil the works of the Holy Spirit: i.e., rejects the source of truth and salvation), it will not be forgiven him, either in this world, or the world to come" (Matthew 12:31-37).

The above passage indicates that there will be certain sins forgiven in the world to come, in the way God has provided.

"The fire will assay the quality of every man's work . . if his work burns (poor quality, i.e., involved no true effort and sacrifice), then he shall lose his reward, but he himself will be saved, yet so as through fire". (I Corinthians 3:13-15).

"In which He (Christ) went and preached to those spirits that were in prison. These in times past had been disobedient" (1 Peter 3:13-20).

". . . the gospel was preached even to the dead . . ." (1 Peter 4:6) if the dead were in hell, why preach to them?

Putting together the promise of Christ and the Holy Spirit so that we cannot be misled on matters of faith and morals, the teaching authority of the Church states clearly that there is indeed a place and way of cleansing a soul from less severe sin or punishment due to sin. This place we call purgatory. We on earth can lessen the burden on these souls by offering our prayers and sacrifices in their name.

Those who have willingly rejected God and His mercy, by serious (mortal) sin and are unrepentant will condemn themselves to everlasting punishment, and these are beyond our help in any way. Those who are saved and cleansed are in God's kingdom and do not need our help. On the final Day of Judgment, all cleansing will have been completed and there will be only heaven and hell. In the CCC, under "The Final Purification #1030 to 1032, we learn the following:

- Christians have a duty to pray for the dead such as deceased relatives, friends, and all the faithful departed.

- Each individual has an awesome responsibility for his or her eternal destiny. The importance of the individual judgment after death, of the refining and purifying passage through purgatory, of the dreadful possibility of eternal death, which is hell, of the last judgment — all should be understood in light of Christian hope.

- At the last judgment, all people will fully reach their eternal destiny. The lives of all are to be revealed before the tribunal of Christ so that "each one may receive his recompense, good or bad, according to his life in the body" (2 Corinthians 5:10). Then, "the evildoers shall rise to be damned," and "those who have done right shall rise to live" (John 5:29): a life eternally with God beyond what the human heart can imagine, a life of eternal enjoyment of the good things prepared by God for those who love Him.

8 – SATAN AND HIS DOCTRINE

Currently, in the public re-affirmation of our baptismal vows, it is not unusual for the minister to leave out the part by which we revoke Satan and all his pomp, etc., and replace it simply by saying, *"we renounce all that is evil."*

In one sense, this is a small thing, but theologically, it is very significant.

Would it be correct to say simply that we are saved by "all that is good" even if in the back of our minds we equate all that is good as coming from God?

I do not think so, as scripture and Church teach that we are saved only by the person of our Lord and Savior Jesus Christ, and what He did for us on the cross. All of that which we call "good," if it is separated from Christ, will not save us.

Since the earliest writings of scripture, and the earliest teaching of the Church, the person of Satan is acknowledged. In our prayer to St. Michael, the archangel, we ask him to "be our safeguard against the wickedness and snares of the Devil," and we ask God that He thrust into hell "Satan and all of the evil spirits who roam through the world seeking the ruin of souls."

Has the teaching on Satan and evil spirits changed with Vatican II?

No, it has not!

Austin Flannery, O.P., as general editor of "Vatican Collection, Volume 2, of Vatican Council II, Post Consiliar Document," in the chapter on Demonology, discusses that some contemporary (modernist?) views would abolish the teaching that Satan and evil spirits exist. And then he goes on to clarify what is the Church teaching in this statement:

"The conclusion is therefore inescapable. That Satan, whom Jesus attacked with His exorcisms and confronted in the wilderness and in His passion, cannot be simply a product of the human ability to tell stories and personify ideas, nor a stray survival of a primitive culture and its language."

In his discussion "B. The Pauline Writings," he states,

Moreover, Paul does not identify sin with Satan. He sees sin first and foremost for what it really is in its essence: a personal human act leading to that state of sin and blindness into which Satan desires to bring and keep men." Paul thus clearly distinguishes Satan from sin. Satan assuredly leads men into sin, but he is himself distinct from the evil he leads them to do.

This statement surely implies that in our baptismal vows, simply saying that "we reject all that is evil" is inadequate.

There is indeed an evil spirit-person who is identified as the "devil," or "Satan," who was "originally good and filled with light," but unfortunately, did not persevere in the true faith in which he was created, but rebelled against the Lord. The evil, therefore, came not from his nature, but from a contingent act of his free will.

St. Paul also identifies Satan as "the evil spirit," saying he functions by inspiring teachers to bring us false doctrines. These instruments for evil become false prophets disguising themselves as apostles of Christ, just as Satan himself disguises himself as "an angel of light." (How many of our dissenting theologians and teachers who disguise themselves as "angels of light" are really confusing us with the doctrine of Satan?).

1 John 4:1 warns all teachers who believe that they are being led by "the Spirit, to make sure that our inspiration is coming from God, not the "evil spirit."

"Beloved, believe not every spirit, but try the spirits whether they are of God: because many false prophets are gone out into the world."

St. Paul gives us three simple guidelines to identify the teachers inspired by the Holy Spirit (most dissenters ignore all three):

1. Do they go to the men of authority (the Magisterium of the Church) as St. Paul did, to verify their teaching (Galatians l & 2; Acts 15:8-12; Acts 16:4).
2. Are they teaching the crucified Christ, i.e., that we can be saved only by what Christ did for us on the cross (l Corinthians 1:23).
3. Are they trying to please men or please God, i.e., do they teach we must change and obey God's law (Galatians 1:10).

In conclusion, if we sin, we become more like Satan, and if we do not repent, we become one of "his own." If we follow the doctrine of Christ, the doctrine of the cross, then we become more like Christ, and one of "His own."

Satan disguises his teaching so that it "looks like" an acceptable teaching, but in essence, is quite the opposite to truth.

The Teachings of Satan

"If there is a God, He has no direct relationship to man.

Therefore, there is no revelation from God to man, i.e., the Bible is ONLY the "experience" of some man or some community. Therefore, the experience of man or the community today equals the Bible as one commandment equals the other."

This is the basic concept of LIBERATION THEOLOGY. Therefore, if the community experience (whatever that is) tells us that divorce and remarriage is okay, that abortion is okay, that homosexuality is okay, that artificial birth control, fornication, masturbation, and adultery are okay — then they are okay! Satan's Doctrine in Regard To Original Sin

"There really is no original sin! Theologians say that God could, not create an imperfect soul, so this soul does not need to be saved."

This may well be the most demonic of his teachings, because, if it were true, then there would be no need for Christ!!! Satan's Doctrine as to Why Christ Came.

Satan cannot deny that Christ did exist, but he cannot acknowledge that Christ is necessary for salvation; therefore, he has to explain away this truth, and he does so by replacement psychology, i.e., giving you a substitution. Satan's explanation for Christ is *"that he came to experience (that word again) our needs and to respond to these needs."*

COMMUNITY becomes the center of the church rather than CHRIST; therefore, community is the authority, the teacher, etc. (Note: Community is why the Church exists. But Christ, His doctrine, His authority, His ways and means of sanctifying MUST be the center and guiding force of that community for it to be called "Catholic.")

Satan's Doctrine as to Baptism

This sacrament has existed since Christ, and cannot be ignored, so here, rather than use replacement psychology, Satan uses a partial truth as a complete truth, i.e., *"Baptism is your initiation into Community,"* and that is all that it is.

In other words, baptism is like joining a club.

The rest of what baptism is and does is ignored, i.e., your adoption into the Family of Christ, the forgiveness of original sin (remember, it does not exist), and forgiveness of all sin, the sharing of all of Christ's teaching, authority and sanctification. (Not teaching

63

a complete truth can be as demonic as teaching a lie.)

All of Satanic doctrine given here is part of what is called "Liberation Theology" or "Modernism" or "Humanism." The essence of Satan's teaching by his followers today is this: *"You are an adult, and can make up your own mind, you do not need any set of rules — decide by what you think — not by what God knows."*

9 – ADDITIONAL THOUGHTS ON CATHOLICS AND PROTESTANTS

True Christian Protestant Theology does indeed accept the doctrine of God, original sin, Christ as Lord and Savior, the necessity of Baptism, and that the Bible is the revealed Word of God.

The difference in a True Christian Protestant and a Catholic is that in addition to what they believe, <u>we also believe:</u>

1. In the Priesthood of the Catholic Church as a continuation of the Priesthood of Christ.
2. In addition to the sacraments of Baptism and Matrimony, we believe that Christ also instituted other Sacraments; i.e., Holy Orders, Holy Eucharist, Reconciliation (Confession), Extreme Unction (anointing of the sick) and Confirmation. (Some Protestant churches do accept some or all of these Sacraments).
3. The real, essential difference is that any person who is truly a Catholic accepts that he who validly follows in the succession of Peter (i.e., the Pope) does have final authority from Christ, by the action and guidance of the Holy Spirit, on matters of "Faith" (what we believe) and "Morals" (our conduct).

Therefore, we believe that Christ is the Invisible Head of our Church, and acts through our visible head, the Pope. Thus, what comes from the Pope as "infallible" (ex-Cathedra) teaching, or as "authoritative teaching," is NOT coming from some man in Rome, but is actually coming from Jesus Christ THROUGH that man in Rome.

Anyone who does not accept this should not identify himself as "Roman Catholic."

The Council of Vatican II gives us a clear and decisive statement as to our obligation to accept the teachings of the Holy Father on faith and morals.

"The Roman Pontiff, head of the college of bishops, enjoys this infallibility in virtue of his office, when, as supreme pastor and teacher of all the faithful – who confirms his brethren in the faith (Luke 22:32) – he proclaims in an absolute decision a doctrine pertaining to faith or morals. For that reason his definitions are rightly said to be irreformable by their very nature and not by reason of

the assent of the Church, in as much as they were made with the assistance of the Holy Spirit promised to him in the person of blessed Peter himself; and as a consequence they are in no way in need of the approval of others, and do not admit of appeal to any other tribunal For in such a case the Roman Pontiff does not utter a pronouncement as a private person, but rather does he expound and defend the teaching of the Catholic faith as the supreme teacher of the universal Church, in whom the Church's charism of infallibility is present in a singular way (Dogmatic Constitution on the Church, Chapter III, #25, Nov. 12. 1964).

This article further reminds us that we are to be guided by our bishops "who are in union with the Pope, the Bishop of Rome, the Vicar of Christ" and those who are "teaching in communion with the Roman Pontiff."

In his statement to our bishops, when he visited the USA in 1988, the Holy Father reminded our bishops, "It is sometimes claimed that dissent from the Magisterium is totally compatible with being a 'Good Catholic' and poses no obstacle to the reception of the sacraments. This is a grave error that challenges the teaching office of the Bishops of the United States and elsewhere."

Council of Vatican II: There have been twenty-one Ecumenical Councils over the past 2000 years, and they have all functioned to do two things: 1. Clarify what is truth, and; 2. Indicate how the message and sanctification be brought to us in the most effective and meaningful way.

No council has ever changed what the Church is or what it does; though they have frequently changed "ways" of doing things! Though some would have you believe otherwise, the post council of Vatican II Church has the same structure, sacraments and dogmas as the pre-Vatican II Church. Vatican II did relax certain disciplines, gave a broader interpretation to certain laws, and changed the way of administering certain sacraments, etc., but what the Church is, i.e., "Christ incarnate in the World," and what the Church is supposed to be doing, i.e., bringing the teaching, authority and sanctification to the world – HAS NOT CHANGED, nor can it!

The first commandment of our Lord to His Apostles was to "COME" with me that I may teach you, guide you and sanctify you. His last command was that they "GO" and make disciples... baptize them . . . "teach them to observe all that I have commanded you."

Therefore, one of the mandatory commands of Our Lord was to teach ALL. In his Exhortation on Catechesis, Pope John Paul II interprets this to mean that of all the obligations of our bishops, priests, and all who teach in the name of Catholicism, their teaching be "not fragmented. but complete," be "not opinionated or confused but in certainty," be "that which is the teaching of the Magisterium (teaching authority) of the Church." If my intent was less than this, I would be more fearful of judgment than had I been a Hitler, as he was responsible only for the death of bodies, and I would be responsible for the loss of souls.

Perhaps the greatest evil in the Church and Christendom today is ignorance — ignorance of original sin and all sin, our need for Christ, "and Christ Crucified," and for what is the true and complete teaching of Christ as given through His one, holy, apostolic, Catholic Church.

We do not follow the teachings of the Church as a puppy follows its master. We follow the teaching of the Church — as thinking adults who know Christ as Lord and Savior, and know that His teaching comes to us THROUGH His Church. It is NOT some man in Rome who is teaching, but it is Christ giving his teaching THROUGH that man in Rome.

We cannot be "cafeteria-style Christians" who pick and choose what we will accept. If we can reject any part of Church teaching, then we can reject ALL of Church teaching, and then we really have no Church, no continuation of Christ in the world, and this would make Satan very happy. Final Thought

Why so many dissident theologians and different Christian religions, and yet we all agree on so many basic beliefs and essentially accept the same Bible?

Is it not because the founder of each religious group felt that they, above all others, were inspired by the Holy Spirit to know the intent of God from the words that were written?

"Many things I have yet to say to you. . . , but when he, the Spirit of Truth comes, he will teach you all truth" (John 16:12).

The problem with the understanding of this passage is that it was said at the Last Supper when ONLY the twelve apostles were present as the leaders of His Church; this is applied primarily to them as His Church leaders, not to each and every one of us individually. On an individual basis the only one given authority to interpret and apply His teaching was to St. Peter (Matthew 16:16-20).

St. Paul reminds us *"The things of God no one knows but the spirit of God . . . these things we (the Church) teach, not words taught by human wisdom, but in the learning of the spirit."* (1 Corinthians 2:11-13)

Some disciples of Satan even question the authenticity and accuracy of the Bible relating to what Christ said and did because the New Testament was not even started until thirty years after the death of Our Lord.

My reply to them is simple: at family gatherings, it is very common for brothers and sisters and family to relate and agree to the accuracy of events and words spoken thirty, forty and fifty years ago, and this without the inspiration and guidance of the Holy Spirit. Remember also that immediately after the death and Ascension of Our Lord, the apostles and disciples went to all parts of the known world and though separated by weeks and months of communication time, their writings about Our Lord and His teaching were amazingly in agreement.

Finally, I repeat dear reader that just as there is the Holy Spirit bringing us everything, which is Christ, there is also the evil spirit, and we must always use our judgment if the person or the message is coming from the Holy Spirit or the evil spirit. It is so important that I want to repeat that St. Paul gives us three basic guidelines to make our judgment:

1. Are they teaching the "crucified Christ?" i.e., we cannot be saved by anything that we or our community are, but only by what Christ did for us on the cross (1 St. John 1:7; 4:1-7; 1 Corinthians 1:23).
2. Are they giving you the teaching accepted by "the men of authority?" (Galatians, Chapters 1 and 2; Acts 15: 6-12; Acts 15:30-31; Acts 16:4).
3. "Are they trying to please men, or trying to please God?" (Galatians 1).

Many who call themselves Catholic dissent from Church teaching fail on all three!

10 – WHY BE A CATHOLIC?
SUMMATION OF CATHOLIC TEACHING

Do not be a Catholic just because you were born a Catholic or raised a Catholic. Be a Catholic because you have prayerfully investigated and studied what the Catholic Church really is its origin, its history, its teaching.

Be a Catholic because:

- It is the only Christian church that can trace its origin, its teaching, its priesthood and authority in an unbroken line back to the twelve apostles and Christ. It was the only Christian church for over 1500 years.
- It is the only church that continues in the fullness of Christ; all of His Teaching, all of His Sacraments, all of His authority.
- It is the only church whose teaching is consistent with the Holy Bible and teaches the full Bible; it does not pick and choose some parts and ignore other parts.
- It interprets the Bible more literally than any other church: The Bible says we may not divorce and remarry and the Church says we may not divorce and remarry; the Bible says that Jesus would give us His Body to eat and His Blood to drink, and the Church says that at the Last Supper and at each "memorial of the Last Supper" (the Mass) He gives us His Body to eat and His Blood to drink; the Bible says that Jesus told His Apostles that they could forgive sins and "they would be forgiven" (John 20: 21-23), and the Church says that His Apostles (and those who are ordained through the apostleship (Acts 1, 15, 26) can forgive sins.

1) Bible Quotations All Catholics Should Be Able To Explain

The place to begin to understand the Church, what it is and its teaching, is the Holy Bible. All Church teaching fits hand and glove with Holy Scripture. As Pope Paul VI reminded us "ignorance of the Bible is ignorance of Christ" and "ignorance of Christ is ignorance of the one Church that was founded, structured and sanctified by the person of Christ."

All of scripture is important, but certain key scriptural quotations should be well memorized and understood so as to act as anchor points for specific and general Church teaching.

First, let us quote some general guidelines the *Catechism of the Catholic Church* (CCC) that we as Catholics must accept.

The CCC especially in Article 3; II, 105 clearly states the Church's position that the Bible is indeed revelation from God. It also strongly encourages all Catholics to read and study the Holy Bible . . . "The Church "forcefully and specifically exhorts all the Christian faithful . . . to learn 'the surpassing knowledge of Jesus Christ,' by frequent reading of the divine Scriptures'" (Article 3,V; 133). The CCC also states that there is no new revelation ". . . there will be no other word than this one" (Article 1; III, 65). i.e., no "experience" in the Church today can in any way change, subtract or add to that which is Holy Scripture, in this sense.

2) Interpretation Of Holy Scripture

In I Corinthians 2: 11-13), St. Paul taught us that...

"The things of God no one knows but the spirit of God. These things we also speak, not in words taught by human wisdom, but in the learning of the spirit."

Therefore, we who are Catholic look to this teaching authority of the Church for knowledge of what was intended by God in revelation, "critical scholarship of itself is not the ultimate source of full interpretation of the sacred texts. This interpretation is the gift of the Holy Spirit given to the Church and guarded by the Magisterium. Everyone who is Catholic must reject any teaching by a "theologian or a Bible scholar" that is not consistent with the teaching of the Church, as they have only the "human wisdom," whereas the Church has had "the learning of the spirit for 2000 years."

3) Importance Of Doctrine

Jesus Himself warns us that unless we hear His word (learn His doctrine), and live His word, we will be "washed away and utterly destroyed" (Matthew 7:24-27).

We cannot be certain that we are following the doctrine of Christ unless we know what is His doctrine. Satan is most happy when one calls himself a Christian, but teaches and follows his (Satan's) doctrine.

"The Church of the Living God, the pillar and mainstay of truth"(I Timothy 3:15).

"If anyone teaches otherwise and does not agree with the sound instruction of Our Lord Jesus Christ and that doctrine...he is proud, knowing nothing"(I Timothy 6: 3-5).

"Who does not abide in the doctrine of Christ, has not God"(2 John 8:11).

St. Paul chastises those who claim to have the "wisdom" of man. (The dissenting theologian and others who refuse to accept, and who attack the teachings of the Church and the Holy Father always quote other dissenters like themselves who have only the wisdom of man and not the "learning of the Holy Spirit" as promised to the teaching authority of the Church).

"That your faith might rest not on the wisdom of man, but on the power of God"(I Corinthians 2:1,9).

"Even so, the things of God no one knows but the spirit of God . . .these things we teach, not in words taught by human wisdom, but in the learning of the spirit"(I Corinthians 2:11,13).

Faith is a gift from God, but to retain that faith we must have knowledge of Christ and His teachings (Matthew 7:21-27).

"Faith depends on hearing the words of Christ"(Romans 10:14-17).

4) Authority Of Peter

In the Old Testament, God changed men's names to identify a position. He changed Abram (Honored Father) to Abraham (Honored Father to the multitude). Even today, he is called Abraham, father. Jacob was changed to Israel (seed); his descendants are called Israelites.

Christ identifies himself as "The Rock," and then Christ changes Simon's name to "Cephas," which is interpreted to mean "Rock" or "Peter," to identify his position (John 1:24).

In Matthew 16:18-20, it says:

"You are the rock, and upon this rock I will build my church. What you bind I will bind . . . what you loose I will loose" (i.e., your decision will be my decision).

In John 21:15-17, Christ identifies Himself as the Good Shepherd, and then transfers this title to Peter. "Feed my lambs . . . feed my lambs . . . feed my sheep," i.e., you are the shepherd.

In Acts 15:6-12, Peter identifies his authority, and then uses it to make the decision on circumcision.

"I remind you, Christ chose me, that through my mouth shall come the words to the gentiles that they may believe."

Paul accepts this authority in Acts 16:4, and in Galatians, Chapters

1 and 2:"1 first went to the men of authority to verify my teaching."
Matthew 18:15-18 shows clearly that what the Church shall bind,
Christ will bind.

For 2,000 years, Catholics have accepted that whoever follows
in the succession of St. Peter continues in this authority given by
Christ to Peter. Linus was the head of the Church after Peter, then
came Cletus, Clement, Sixtus, etc., down to John Paul II (all except
three are buried beneath St. Peter's in Rome).

5) Priesthood

The words directed to the apostles at the Last Supper by
Christ, and in many other places in scripture, clearly indicate that
Christ intended to institute the priesthood:

*"Amen, Amen, I say to you, he who receives anyone I
send, receives Me" (John 13:20).*

*"You have not chosen Me, but I have chosen you and
have appointed you so that you should go and bear fruit,
and that your fruit shall remain" (John 15:16).*

*"Because you are not of the world, But I have chosen
you out of the world" (John 15:19)*

*"And I am no longer in the world, but these are in the
world" (John 17:11).*

*"And the world hated them because they are not of the
world, even as I am not of the world" (John 17:14).*

*"Even as thou has sent me into the world, so I also
have sent them into the world" (John 17:18).*

*"That all may be one, even as Thou Father, in Me and
I in Thee" (John 17:21).*

"That they may be perfected in unity" (John 17:23).

*On the day of His Resurrection, Christ said TO His
Apostles,*

*"As the Father has sent Me, I also send you." When
He had said this, He breathed upon them and said to
them . . . Receive the Holy Spirit, whose sins you shall
forgive, they are forgiven them, and whose sins you
retain, they are retained" (John 20:21-23).*

The apostles were ordained to be an "extension" of the priesthood of Christ — not "another" priest. The apostles understood that
they had the authority to pass this priesthood on from one to another when they chose Matthias to take the place of Judas "as one of
the 12 apostles," i.e., apostolic succession (Acts 1:15-26). (Only the

apostles, i.e., the bishops, have the fullness of the priesthood and can ordain others into the priesthood. The apostles "ordained" assistants, i.e., presbyters, which we now call priests, with a limited power of the priesthood to teach and administer certain sacraments, etc.; and the deacon to assist in other Church duties — Acts 6:1,7; Acts 1:5,6).

6) Confession Or Reconciliation

"Whose sins you forgive, they are forgiven them, etc." (John 20:21-23). The apostles are given the power and authority to forgive sins.

"Confess your sins to one another" (James 5:15).

For 2,000 years, Catholics have been confessing their sins to those who are the continuation of the apostles, i.e., a priest or a bishop. By confessing or telling their sins, they are asking Christ, through this priest, to accept their burden of sin, onto His Cross, to be washed in His blood, i.e., to be justified or cleansed. Christ wants us to hand Him our sins personally, not throw them out into the empty void of space.

7) The Holy Eucharist

At the Last Supper, in Matthew, Mark and Luke, the Holy Eucharist is instituted by Christ through the Words, "This is my body . . . this is my blood." You (my priest) do this in commemoration of Me."

Christ gives a dissertation which goes on for fifty verses, repeating in ten different ways that He will give us His Flesh to eat and His Blood to drink (John 6:22-72).

We must eat and drink of Christ's body and blood to have HIS life in us. (When the Jews understood that Christ literally meant what He said, they all left Him, except Peter and the apostles, who did not understand it but accepted it in faith!)

"Therefore, whoever eats this bread or drinks this cup
of the Lord unworthily will be guilty of sins against the
body and blood of the Lord" (I Corinthians 11:23-30).

St. Paul understood this to be the living "body and blood" of Christ.

For 2,000 years, Catholics have believed that at the Last Supper and at every repetition of the Last Supper (the Mass), bread and wine are changed into the body and blood of Our Lord. We do not understand it, but believe it because we have faith in HIS words! Could Christ do any less than truly be with us and in us?

The Mass is clearly documented in Acts 2:42:

"And they continued steadfastly in the teaching of the Apostles and in the Communion of the breaking of the bread and in prayers."

Today, we are somewhat more formal, but the Mass still is exactly the same as it was 2,000 years ago.

"And upon the first day of the week, when the disciples came together to break bread, Paul preached unto them, ready to depart on the morrow; and continued his speech until midnight" (Acts 20:7).

They performed this ritual at least once a week, on "the first day," which they called "The Lord's Day;" and the Church has continued to keep holy this "Lord's Day" since the time of the apostles. In I Corinthians 2:23-26, St. Paul uses essentially the same words as the priest uses today; it is a re-enactment of the Last Supper.

8) Baptism

"Go teach all nations, baptizing them in the name of the Father, the Son, and the Holy Spirit" (John 3:5-7); also Matthew 28:18-20.

"Unless you are born again of the water and the spirit, you shall not enter into the Kingdom of Heaven" (Mark 16:15).

Catholics truly believe that when we are baptized, we are literally adopted into the family of Christ, are cleansed of all sin, and given an inheritance into everything that is Christ. It is our initiation into community but is also far more than that.

The Church has always taught that baptism is necessary for salvation.

"Therefore through one man, sin entered the "world...has passed to all men" (Romans 5:12-14).

The blood of Jesus cleanses us from sin (I John 1:7-8). Without the shedding of blood, there is no forgiveness of sin (Hebrews 9:22-28).

"If we say that we have not sinned, we make Him a liar, and His word is not in us" (I John 1:10).

"We know that whosoever is born of God sinneth not; but he that is begotten of God keepeth himself, and that wicked one toucheth him not" (I John 5:18).

"Faith depends on hearing, and on hearing the Word of Christ" (Romans 10:17).

Perhaps the most serious sin of all is to deny original sin, because then we deny the need of a Savior, and the need for baptism. Baptism, then, would become only our initiation into a club or group.

9) Divorce

"What God has joined together, let no man put asunder"(Mark 10:2).

"Whoever puts away his wife and marries another commits adultery" (Mark 10:12).

"And he who marries a woman who has been put away commits adultery"(Luke 16:18).

"If a woman departs from her husband...she is to remain unmarried or be reconciled to her husband" (I Corinthians 7:10-11).

It is not the Church that has made these laws!

Christ instituted these laws and if we are to continue as the Church of Christ, we must continue in these teachings on divorce! Yes, at times it is very difficult to abide by this law commanded by Christ; but it is God's law, and each of us —society in general and children in particular— would greatly benefit if we as unselfish, mature adults approached marriage in this state of commitment.

10) Lying, Or False Teachers, Or Dissident Theologians

Lying, false teachers and dissident theologians cause confusion within the Church (I Timothy 6:3-5; 2 Timothy 3:1-9).

"Beloved, believe not every spirit, but try the spirits whether they are of God: because many false prophets are gone out into the world.

"But knew ye the Spirit of God: Every spirit that confesseth that Jesus Christ is come in the flesh is of God:" (I John 4:1-2).

"Do not be led away by various and strange doctrines" (Hebrews 13:7).

"Watch those who cause dissension . . . contrary to doctrine...they serve their own belly" (Romans 16:17).

2 Peter 2: read entire chapter, especially verses 17 to 19:

"They are springs without water . . . they promise them freedom, whereas they themselves are the slaves of corruption:"

"Do not use freedom as a cloak for vice" (1 Peter 2:17).

"Anyone who advances and does not abide in the doctrine of Christ has not God . . . do not receive him into your house or say to him Welcome . . . then you share in his evil works" (2 John 8:11).

"Professing to be wise, they have become fools" (Romans 1:22).

Read the introduction to the Epistle of St. Jude; it is directed against those who oppose all law and authority.

"These men also defile the flesh, disregard authority . . . haughty in speech . . . walking according to their lust...set themselves apart" (Jude 5:19).

St. Paul voices stem condemnation to those who are preaching other doctrines:

"But even if we or an angel from heaven should preach a gospel to you other than that which we have preached to you, let him be anathema."

"For am I seeking to please God...or man" (Galatians 1:6-10).

Today, many teachers are bringing us "false doctrines." We must know our faith or lose it!

11) The Commandments

Jesus said,

"But if thou will enter into eternal life, keep the Commandments" (Matthew 19:16-22). Which ones? All of them!

Also covered in Luke 10:25-30.

"I have not come to destroy the Law or the Prophets . . . but to fulfill . . . whoever does away with one of these least Commandments, and so teaches men, shall be called least" (Matthew 5:17-22).

We must love God above all else, and our neighbors as our/selves. However, this law of Love does not replace the Commandments, rather it fulfills them (Mark 12:28-34).

"If you love Me, keep My Commandments" (John 14:15).

"He who has MY Commandments and keeps them, he it is who loves me" (John 14:21).

"If anyone loves Me, he will keep My word (John 14:23).

For 2,000 years, Catholics have believed that Christ poured out into His apostles His own spirit of love and forgiveness of sin, so that they became "an extension of Himself." Christ Himself, working through them, changes bread and wine into His own body 'and blood, and through them takes the burden of our sins onto Himself on the cross.

Therefore, He is not a God "way out there," but rather a very personal God who wants to touch us in a one-to-one relationship. When we are "touched by Christ" in this one-to-one personal relationship, and the appropriate sign is present, we call this a "sacrament," i.e., a "sacred moment" when we are personally "touched" by Our Lord.

Also, the priesthood does not come from man or by man or community, but only from God through the apostleship of Christ.

12) God Works Through Holy Things

"And God worked more than the usual miracles by the hand of Paul so that even handkerchiefs and aprons were carried from his body to the sick, and the disease left them and the evil spirits went out" (Acts 19:11-12).

SUMMATION OF OUR FAITH

God: We know that God exists because of creation, miracles, and fulfilled prophecies; one God, three divine persons. Bible: We know that it is God's word because of miracles, fulfilled prophecies and the words of Christ Himself in reference to teachings, commandments, happenings, etc., of the Old Testament.

Christ: We know Christ is "The Messiah, Son of God, God Himself" because of miracles; His conception, life and death were foretold in biblical prophecies, as was His RESURRECTION; also, through his own proclamations, he acknowledged He was Christ.

Mary: The ever virgin, mother of Christ; the most perfect of all of God's creations. In all of scripture, she is the only human called "Blessed."

Reason for Christ: He came to teach us what we must know about God and His Kingdom — we call them matters of faith: and He came to teach us what our conduct must be toward our bodies! and each other — we call them matters of morals.

Christ came to guide us, give us definitive guidelines and authority so we would not be led astray. He came to sanctify us — cleanse us of our sins and make us worthy to be in His Kingdom.

Reason for Church: Christ wished that this teaching, authority and sanctification continue in the world and throughout the whole world for all time. So, He structured His Church with the twelve apostles as an extension of Himself in His teaching; He gave the Church, the sacraments, and the priesthood, an extension of Himself, in sanctifying us; He gave us St. Peter as an extension of His authority so that we would not be led astray.

And finally, He promised to us that the Holy Spirit would guide and guard this Church for all time (St. John 14:15-21; St. John 15:26; St. John 16:12-16).

Although glorified now at the right hand of the Father, the Lord Jesus remains in the world through the Church, "His Body."

"Even as thou has sent me into the world, so I have also sent them into the world. And for them I sanctify myself, that they also may be sanctified in truth; yet not only for these do I pray, but for those also who through their words are to believe in me, that all may be one, even as thou Father in me, and I in Thee, that they may also be one in us . . . that they be one, even as we are .

. . that they may be perfected in unity. Trust is unity — the one mark of truth is that it is one" (John 17:14-26).

We certainly must acknowledge that there are different ways of expressing one truth (different viewpoints, i.e., acceptable pluralism); however, we must always be alert that some so-called "different viewpoints" are not really "different doctrines."

The Holy Spirit: Christ founded, structured, taught and sanctified His Church so that it would be a continuation of Himself in the world.

But the Church did not go anywhere.

There was not one sermon or one conversion until the Holy Spirit came upon them.

The Holy Spirit, then, is the energizing and guiding force in the Church and brings to us all that is Christ. At the Last Supper, Our Lord said to His apostles "The Holy Spirit will teach you all things...he will declare to you what is mine."

We see, then, that the blessed Trinity — one God, and three divine persons — functions in an individual yet "collective way."

God the Father is Creator, and creation still goes on with each new soul; God the Son is our way (our only way) of redemption and salvation (and creation would be meaningless if 'we had no way of salvation); God the Holy Spirit brings to us all that is our salvation (without Him the Church would cease to function).

Is the Church biblical in its structure?

Does it have bishops? (Apostolic succession to the apostles.)

Does it have priests? (Presbyters who are a continuation of the priesthood of Christ.) (Acts 15, 6.)

Does it have deacons? (Acts 6.)

Does it have one whom the early church recognized as being in authority by appointment of Christ? (Acts 15.)

Yes it does, and has so functioned since the time of Christ! Does it demand that we accept the teaching of Christ literally on divorce & remarriage; obeying the commandments; forgiveness of sin through its priest; bringing us the Body and Blood of Christ, so that He can be with us and in us, as Jesus commanded at the Last Supper; and that He continues in the world, in and through His church, <u>His Body?</u>

Yes it does.

11 – YOUR JOURNEY HAS NOT ENDED!

As you near the end of this little pilgrim's journey, you have had much to absorb. I pray that God has blessed you as you read this book and that it has given you a deeper understanding of the Catholic Church.

But, this book by no means finishes your search for complete answers; it hopefully served to simply stimulate you on to further study.

Your journey has just begun! Remember that there is nothing more vital than the decisions and study you undertake now; it has eternal implications for your soul.

I repeat the words of our Lord:

"I have not come to judge you or condemn you. . . but to save you. . . He who rejects me, and does not accept my words, has one to condemn him" John 12:44-48).

"If I had not come and spoken to them (to you), you would have no sin. But now you have no excuse for your sin" John 15:22).

The books I most heartily recommend for further study on your journey are:

CATECHISMS:

Catechism of the Catholic Church, St. Paul, The Wander Press, 1994.

Baltimore Catechism #3, Connell, Fr. Francis J., Colorado Springs, The Seraphim Company, Inc., 1991.

The Catholic Catechism, John A. Hardon, S.J., Garden City, NY, Doubleday & Co., Inc., 1975.

PATROLOGY:

The Faith of the Early Fathers, Jurgens, H.E.D., William A., Collegeville, The Liturgical Press, 1970.

Patrology, Quasten, Johannes, Westminister, Christian Classics, Inc., 1990.

APOLOGETICS:

"Essay on the Development of Christian Doctrine," Newman, John Henry, Notre Dame, Notre Dame Press, 1989.

The Catholic Controversy, De Sales, St. Francis, Rockford, Tan Books and Publishers, Inc., 1989.

Catholicism and Fundamentalism, Keating, Karl, San Francisco, Ignatius Press, 1988.

MISCELLANEOUS:

The Catholic Faith, Hardon, S.J., John A., Editor, Ignatius Press

The Catholic Lifetime Reading Plan, Hardon, S.J., John A., New York, Doubleday, 1989.

What Does Scripture Say?, Tom Balboa and Joseph C. Bonadiman, San Bernardino,CA, Catholic Society of Evangelist, 2000.

Summa Theologica, St. Thomas Aquinas, New York, Benziger Brothers, 1947.

Fundamentals of Catholic Dogma, Dr. Ludwig Ott, Rockford, Tan Books & Publishers, Inc., 1974.

Vatican Council II, Boston, Daughters of St. Paul, 1975.

The Canons and Decrees of the Council of Trent, Rockford, Tan Books & Publishers, Inc., 1941.

An Essay on the Development of Christian Doctrine, John Henry Cardinal Newman, Notre Dame, Notre Dame Press, 1989.

Reading in Church History, Westminister, MD, Christian Classics, Inc., 1985.

Radio Replies, The Rev. Dr. Leslie Rumble, MSC & Rev Charles Mortimer Carthy, Rockford, Tan Books & Publishers, Inc., 1938.

Confessions of St. Augustine, Union City, John J. Crawley & Co., 1979.

PUBLISHERS:

Tan Books, P. O. Box 424, Rockford, IL. 61105, (800) 437-5876

Ignatius Press, 2515 McAllister St., San Francisco, CA 94118-0390, (415) 387-2324

MAGAZINES:

Envoy Magazine, Subscriber Services, New Hope, KY 40052-9989, (800) 55-ENVOY

Homiletic & Pastoral Review, P. O. Box 591810, San Francisco, CA 94159-1810, (800) 353-2324

The Catholic Answer, Fr. Peter Stravinskas, STD, Ph.D., 200 Noll Plaza, Huntington, IN 46750, (800) 348-2440

St. Joseph's Communications, P. O. Box 720, West Covina, CA 91793,
(626) 331-3549

The Catholic World Report, P. O. Box 591300, San Francisco, CA 94159-1300, (800) 651-1531

Catholic Answers, 2020 Gillespie Way, El Cajon, CA 92020, (619) 387-7200.

Sursum-Corda, P. O. Box 2286, Ft. Collins, CO 80522-2286, (970) 490-2735.

Adoremos, P. O. Box 146, Front Royal, VA 22630

TELEVISION:

The Coming Home Network, P. O. Box 4100, Steubenville, OH 43952,
(614) 283-6320.

EWTN, 5817 Old Leeds Road, Irondale, AL, 35210, (205)271-2900.

By all means, *The Catechism of the Catholic Church* (Libreria Editvice Vaticana) which is THE AUTHORITY as to what is Catholic teaching. Any person who does not accept all of the dogmatic and major doctrinal teaching contained in that Catechism does, in fact, reject the authority from which it comes, the successor of St. Peter and the Church Magisterium; and they must identify themselves or be identified as not a Catholic; and. must not be allowed to teach the Catholic faith in any Catholic institution; or Catholic seminars or lecturer sponsored by any Church authority.

The function of the Holy Spirit in the Church is to bring us all that is Christ and His teaching in a pure and certain way (St. John 16,12,16). The sin against the Holy Spirit *"which will not be forgiven in this life, or the next life"* may well be allowing those to speak in the Church who cause dissension and confusion as to what is the teaching of Christ through the authority of the Church (Matthew 12,32). St. Paul also reminds our Bishops to *"beware of the wolves who will get in among you, and will not spare the flock"* (Acts 20,28,31). St. John also reminds our Bishops *"he who does not abide in the doctrine of Christ, has not God...he who welcomes such a man shares in the evil he does"* (Second Epistle of St. John, vs. 8,11).

Through this book, we hope, the road map is now clearer for you, the worldly distractions are less, and your direction is focused. You know your spiritual destination — eternal life. You know your spiritual road map — the Catholic Church, the Holy Bible, and the revelations handed down through Sacred Tradition.

May God's grace abundantly bless you on the rest of your pilgrim's journey.

IMPLEMENTING THE NEW CATECHISM
By Fr. Kenneth Baker, S.J.
Editor, *Homiletic and Pastoral Review*
(Reprinted with permission from the
Homiletic and Pastoral Review)

The new *Catechism of the Catholic Church* (CCC) is available for purchase and study in English translation. Readers of HPR are already familiar with the structure and basic content of the CCC. I do not think it is necessary for me to try to convince you about the great importance of this amazing book. It is just what the Church needs in this time of crisis. Given the known opposition to the Catechism from dissenters in the field of theology, liturgy and catechetics, the fact that it was produced at all manifests, to me, the guidance of the Holy Spirit and the abiding presence of Our Lord in His Church (Matthew 28:20).

The one point I want to stress in this editorial is the importance of the proper and faithful *implementation* of the Catechism. I say this because there are influential and well-known people in the Catholic Church who are not happy with this Catechism. They will do everything they can to put it on a dusty shelf or ignore it, just as they have ignored previous Vatican documents such as the Pope's letter on the family, *Familiaris Consortio* (1981).

Some have said publicly that they will use it "in their own fashion," that is, they will eliminate most of the solid doctrinal and moral *content* of the Catechism and so "adapt" it to the failed experimental religious instruction of the past twenty-five years. But it is precisely because of the failure of the catechetical establishment to teach the Catholic faith that the Catechism was deemed necessary in the first place!

Implementation of the Catechism on all levels of instruction - that is what we need and that is what each one of us must strive to do in his own way. What I will do is give the proper references to the Catechism after each homily in HPR. The purpose is to urge preachers to consult the Catechism and use it in their homilies. Cardinal O'Connor of New York has said that he will base his weekly Sunday sermons on the Catechism for the next few years. That is a suggestion I would recommend to all priests and bishops.

Cardinal O'Connor has also said that he has directed every

division of the New York Archdiocese to implement the Catechism. I wish every bishop would do that - and then see to it personally that the order is carried out from grade school to university. For the Catechism is too important to turn over to the experts. One does not have to be an "expert," one does not have to possess an advanced degree in religious education in order to read the Catechism or, for that matter to teach it. The Catechism is very clear and easy to understand. That is one reason the experts do not like it.

Who is opposed to the Catechism? I would like my readers to be crystal clear about this point. Dissenters, not only those opposed to *Humanae Vitae*, but those who reject the Church's teaching on such matters as the Holy Sacrifice of the Mass, the Real Presence, Original Sin, the Sacrament of Holy Orders, the ordination of women to the priesthood and so forth - all of these and their followers are opposed, in one way or another to the Catechism. Why? Because the Catechism clearly states for all to see what the truth is and they reject it. Many of them are not really Catholics at all; they pretend to be Catholics for the sake of power, prestige and money.

It is important to realize that there will be a battle over the proper implementation of the CCC. I hope that each one of you will do what you can to get the Catechism into schools, CCD, RCIA and every area of Catholic instruction. As our Pope has said, the Catechism is "a great gift of God" to the Church. It is up to us to implement it.

To order reprints of this book, please contact:

Catholic Society of Evangelists
22797 Barton Road, Suite 117
Grand Terrace, CA 92313 - USA

———

1 BOOK = $5.00
For an AUDIO TAPE (90 Minutes) upon which this book is
based, ADD $2.00 ADDITIONAL.

*For five or more books, add $2.00 per book, plus $1.00 each for each
audio tape - if you wish both.*

———

All persons working with the Society are volunteers, and all money received goes to production and distribution of Orthodox Roman Catholic literature and tapes which are based on the teachings of the Magisterium of the Church as outlined in the Official Catechism of the Catholic Church.

Neither the author nor other workers receive any compensation from the proceeds of these books or tapes.

If you are unable to afford the cost of these books, please write the Catholic Society of Evangelists.